The Motorless Flight Series

THE WILD, WONDERFUL WORLD
OF PARACHUTES AND PARACHUTING

In Preparation

MANBIRDS: Hang Gliders & Hang Gliding
THE GREAT AMERICAN BALLOON BOOK
HALF-A-MILE UP WITHOUT AN ENGINE: Sailplanes & Soaring

The Motorless Flight Series

BUD SELLICK

The Wild, Wonderful World of PARACHUTES AND PARACHUTING

Prentice-Hall, Inc., Englewood Cliffs, New Jersey

Dedicated to Punky

Book Designer: Linda Huber
Art Director: Hal Siegel

The Wild, Wonderful World of Parachutes and Parachuting
by Bud Sellick

Previously published under title: *Parachutes and Parachuting: A Modern Guide to the Sport*

Printed in the United States of America
Prentice-Hall International, Inc., London
Prentice-Hall of Australia, Pty. Ltd., Sydney
Prentice-Hall of Canada, Ltd., Toronto
Prentice-Hall of India Private Ltd., New Delhi
Prentice-Hall of Japan, Inc., Tokyo
Prentice-Hall of Southeast Asia Pt. Ltd., Singapore
Whitehall Books Limited, Wellington, New Zealand

10 9 8 7 6 5 4 3 2 1

Library of Congress Cataloging in Publication Data

Sellick, Bud.
  The wild, wonderful world of parachutes and parachuting.
    (The Motorless flight series)
    Includes index.
    1. Parachuting. I. Title. II. Series: Motorless flight series.
GV770.S443 797.5'6 80-20526
ISBN 0-13-959577-5

Preface

Working the straightened coat hanger carefully down inside my cast, I scratched my swollen leg ever so gently and sighed a sigh of ecstasy. Obviously my first parachute jump was less than a booming success, but I hated to be a quitter so early in the game. Trouble was, the game as we know it today hadn't been invented yet so there were no rules and no sport parachutes. During the following years I kept jumping and getting together with other equally uninformed but highly enthusiastic whuffos. In addition to my impressive collection of plaster casts, Ace bandages, and metal braces, I also collected hundreds of clippings, notes, tape recordings, and firsthand jump experiences. It was more than twenty years ago when I decided to put this information into a book to help others learn about the sport without having to shed blood and break bones in the process. I contacted a dozen publishers, who were mildly amused at the idea of people jumping out of airplanes but rejected the idea of writing a book about it. They expressed doubt that there would ever be enough interest in such a highly specialized subject to warrant a book. One publisher attacked the idea as downright dangerous, saying young people might try it and get themselves killed (that is, "We don't want to get sued!"). But another publisher asked to see an outline, then a few pages, and finally a complete manuscript. They're now publishing this, my third book on the subject.

When I wrote *Skydiving* back in 1960, the sport was just getting started. With a cheap military surplus parachute and a pair of pinking shears, you could design your own sport parachute. When I wrote *Parachutes and Parachuting* in 1971, the round Para-Commander had ruled the sport for six years and the first "squares" were just beginning to win acceptance. Now I see equipment that is half as heavy and twice as strong, that flies twice as fast but descends much more slowly than just a few years ago. Many jumpers who weren't even born when I wrote *Skydiving* have thousands of sport jumps to their credit. Parachutists of today are limited only by their imagination—and as you'll see in this book, some have terrific imaginations.

A few years ago two parachutists under their inflated canopies would avoid each other at all costs, fearing their parachutes would entangle. Now you may see as many as a dozen canopies stacked together in a 300-foot high formation. Not only is the canopy ram-air inflated but some of the jumpsuits are, too. Jumping from airplanes is okay but more and more are taking to parachuting from cliffs, bridges, and buildings. One of that new breed of parachutists is veteran skydiver Carl Boenish, who told me what he sees in the future for parachutists. He envisions the police roping off a two-block area in New York City each Sunday morning and permitting qualified skydivers to jump off the World Trade Center. Don't laugh. At least one person couldn't wait and has already done it!

This book represents an accumulation of information and photographs over many years and the support of hundreds of parachutists. To these people who have helped make our sport and this book possible, my sincere thanks.

A very special recognition goes to the United States Parachute Association and Paul Proctor, editor of *Parachutist*. Mike Truffer of *Skydiving* newsmagazine was generous with his support. Phil Rogge and Paul Hutter of the U.S. Army Parachute Team's Golden Knights were especially cooperative, furnishing information and photographs. A special thanks goes to Jean and Carl Boenish for personal accounts of participation in world record jumps, cliff jumps, and bridge jumps as well as for the use of hundreds of photographs. Ray Cottingham, recognized for years as one of the world's best free-fall photographers, contributed immeasurably. "Old timers" like Lyle Cameron, Ralph White, Joe Gonzales, and the late Bob Buquor furnished limitless support for the original edition. For editorial help above and beyond the call of duty a special salute to Pierce Ellis.

Bud Sellick D-225
Nashville, Tennessee

Contents

1. How It All Began

Our Parachuting Heritage

The *Mona Lisa* of the parachuting world was drawn three years after a fellow Italian discovered America. Leonardo da Vinci did the sketch (shown on page 2) for his *Codex Atlanticus*. Although the force of air was recognized in ancient times and was used to push sailing vessels, Da Vinci was one of the earliest to conceive the idea of air supporting a man's weight. He sketched and made notes about a glider, several flying machines that had flapping wings and relied on muscle power, the retractable landing gear to cut down on drag, a flying saucer with movable wings that resembled oars, an air-screw of the helicopter design, and the parachute pictured here. Of the parachute, he wrote, "If a man have a tent of closely woven linen without any apertures, twelve braccia across and twelve in depth, he can throw himself down from any great height without injury."

The size of Da Vinci's chute is determined by his unit of measure—a *braccio*. The term comes from the Italian word meaning "arm." It is defined as an

Leonardo da Vinci sketched this parachute design in 1495. Although it was never actually constructed, there is every reason to believe it would have worked.

arm's length by some sources; according to various others it ranges from 15 to 39 inches. One source nails it down to exactly 18.4 inches. Using the extremes, his chute was anywhere from 15 to 39 feet square. I don't know about you, but my arm measures 29 inches. Multiply that by twelve *braccia* and you get 348 inches or 29 feet. And a 29-foot square pyramid is 841 square feet of material—enough to safely lower *any* size human being. (The Strato-Cloud sport parachute canopy has approximately 230 square feet of material; the Safety-Flyer reserve has approximately 160 square feet.)

Some sources credit Fausto Veranzio, a hundred years after Da Vinci's sketch was published, with designing and actually jumping his parachute. While it is true that Veranzio drew a picture of a square canvas parachute being used from a tower, there is little evidence to support his claim that he actually jumped with it. In those times (1595) the designer usually gathered a huge crowd around him to watch his initial attempt at anything as dramatic as this since the first attempt was frequently the last attempt.

Other names crop up in various history sources as possibly being the first to make a parachute jump. Joseph Montgolfier, the balloonist and papermaker, claimed to have parachuted from the top of his home in Annonay, France. Sebastien Lenormand, professor of technology at the Paris Conservatory of Arts and Handicrafts, claimed to have parachuted from the Montpelier observatory. In 1785, Jean Pierre Blanchard, the balloonist, experienced difficulty with his over-inflated balloon over Ghent and is credited by some sources as being the first to jump from a balloon. He claimed he broke his leg on that emergency jump and, if he actually made the jump, he also deserves a special notice as receiving the first parachuting injury.

Finally, in 1797, balloonist André Jacques Garnerin made the first of many undisputed exhibition parachute jumps from his balloon. His first was over Paris with thousands watching.

Garnerin's parachute was made of silk with a supporting pole and looked like a huge reinforced umbrella. Standing in a basket at the end of the pole, he released his chute and then oscillated violently as the unvented canopy spilled air first from one side and then from the other. He apparently was sticking to Da Vinci's instructions that the material should be "without any aperture." One source says this first jump was from 8,000 feet, while another says it was from 2,000 feet. Those of us who have jumped the flat circular chutes sympathize with him and hope his jump was from only 2,000 feet.

Sir George Cayley proposed an inverted cone to eliminate objectionable oscillation. He claimed that he built such a chute and that a German, Lorenze Hengler, safely descended from as high as 400 feet on several occasions. Cayley's idea for eliminating oscillation also may be credited with eliminating the first parachutist. The first known parachute fatality took place in 1837 when Robert Cocking took a 5,000-foot plunge in his collapsed, cone-shaped chute. The French astronomer Joseph Lalande is given credit for eliminating a great deal of this oscillation when he suggested a hole in the top to allow a small portion of air to escape, making the canopy more stable. Almost thirty years later the American Captain Thomas Baldwin also advocated the vent in the apex, claiming it helped in slipping or guiding his parachute as well as providing stability.

Until the balloon, there was little opportunity to use a parachute. Ironically, the parachute was used almost exclusively for exhibitions. Although the early balloons were made of treated paper and lifted by the heat of burning straw, the idea of using a parachute for emergencies never came to light. Because parachuting had always been thought of as a stunt, the first lifesaving jump in 1808 was a novelty. Jodaki Kuparento parachuted from his burning balloon over Warsaw. His method of exit and operation of the parachute is unknown.

Normally, before the balloon ascended, the apex of the parachute was attached to the bottom of the balloon's gondola. Strung out beneath the balloon as it ascended were the balloon's gondola, the parachute canopy and lines, and the parachutist in his basket. At the proper height, the balloon's pilot would cut the line that secured the canopy to his ship. The balloon would shoot up and the parachute would drift down.

Jumpers soon found the crowds less enthusiastic when it became apparent the parachute would lower them safely. Exhibition jumpers needed a gimmick. Removing the parachute basket, they substituted a trapeze bar and did all manner of unsafe and insane stunts as the balloon ascended and the parachute descended. This helped, but soon the crowds wanted more.

By the early twentieth century the trapeze bar was becoming passé. Then somebody struck upon the idea of hiding the parachute in a sack and riding up without displaying it to the crowd. The surprise of seeing the man drop free of the balloon for a moment was enough to bring some of the crowds back.

The sack with the parachute folded inside was secured to the balloon's basket. A break cord was attached to the apex of the parachute and to the basket. When the jumper released his trapeze, he would drop, breaking the cord on the sack and allowing lines and canopy to be drawn out. When the chute was completely extended, his weight would break the cord that held the apex of his chute to the basket and he would float free. Since there was now the question of the canopy catching air and inflating, the crowds watched each drop with bloodthirsty anticipation. The hot-air balloon and the parachutist on the trapeze bar became standard items at county fairs, circuses, and other crowd-gathering events through the late 1920's. A few of those daredevils lived to become highly respected sport parachutists. Pictured is Charles E. Dame, former president of the New Hampshire Parachute Club and a United States Parachute Association Area Safety Officer. His cotton parachute is folded neatly above his trapeze as he ascends beneath the hot-air balloon.

While some balloonists and parachutists continued to cavort around the sky thrilling crowds, others were working very seriously on the idea of a heavier-than-air machine that would actually fly.

Sir George Cayley, who designed the inverted-cone parachute to reduce oscillation, earned the title "father of British aeronautics" for other reasons. Fifty-five years before Lenoir completed his first practicable gasoline engine, Cayley had proposed an airplane, propeller-driven by an engine. The problem of flight, he stated, was "to make a surface support a given weight by the application of power to the resistance of air." He constructed a biwinged glider and incorporated into it his theories of initial velocity, wing loads, bending movements, lightness, and strength. He designed it to be as streamlined as possible, using a revolutionary cambered wing—a basic necessity for lift—rather than a flat surface. His biplane was constructed soundly with struts and diagonal bracing, and fitted with horizontal and vertical stabilizers. It flew with a hired hand aboard in

Charles Dame of Rochester, N.H., rides a trapeze aloft under a hot air balloon in 1927. His parachutes are stowed in a sack over his head. On this particular drop, he made a triple drop, cutting away from the first and second chutes to alight with the third—a thrilling show even by modern standards.

1809—almost a hundred years before the Wright brothers' first powered flight.

Orville and Wilbur Wright had scientifically built gliders, testing them in their own laboratories and their own wind tunnel, but gliders had been developed—powered flight had not. Experimenting in powered flight, Otto Lilienthal and Percy Pilcher had killed themselves in crashes. Penniless and frustrated, Alphonse Penaud had committed suicide at the brink of success. Clement Ader, Sir Hiram Maim, and Dr. Samuel Langley had spent many thousands of dollars and utilized the pooled knowledge of the world's greatest aeronautical minds and had failed. The Wright brothers succeeded, however, and powered flight opened new realms for the parachute.

In 1909 the powered airplane was solidly (for that day anyhow) in the aviation picture. The Wright brothers were now regularly flying as much as an hour or more. Glenn Curtiss had build his first plane and was flying it. Glenn Martin had also built a plane and was flying it. Louis Bleriot had flown across the English Channel.

To help finance his aviation enterprises, Glenn Martin staged a demonstration in 1910 and charged spectators to watch him fly his contraption. The demonstration was so successful that he continued to make exhibition flights and charge for them. By 1913 he had discovered that simply keeping his plane aloft was no longer thrilling the people. He needed a gimmick—just as the balloonists a hundred or more years before him had. His gimmick was the parachute. For bonus points, he added sex. Miss Georgia "Tiny" Broadwick, teenage veteran of many drops from hot-air balloons, became the first woman to parachute from an airplane—his Martin hydroplane. Martin built a trap seat alongside the fuselage and rigged the parachute so a static line would open the chute after Tiny slid from her perch.

A year earlier, over Venice, California, Grant Morton had made the first parachute jump from a plane in flight. Carrying the chute folded in his arms, he threw it into the air as he leaped into space. The pilot, Phil Parmalee, was considered to be the one recklessly taking chances, since it was then believed that the sudden loss of the parachutist's weight would throw the plane hopelessly out of control.

That same year, near St. Louis, Captain Albert Berry made the first jump from a plane using the pack-type parachute. The parachute was stowed in a metal container attached to the plane's skid, with a rope extending up to a belt worn by Berry. He climbed down to the axle and at an altitude of 1,500 feet and a speed of 50 mph, dropped away, drawing the parachute from the metal container as he fell. The plane was a Benoist pusher biplane piloted by Anthony Jannus. Here, too, the pilot was taking the chances; but Tony Jannus had already made a name for himself as a daring pilot when he flew a Benoist flying boat 1,970 miles from Omaha to New Orleans—in only 39 days!

When World War I came and the military took over the airplane, it somehow neglected to take over the parachute; after all, the parachute was still nothing more than a stunt man's tool. There was little thought of a pilot trusting his life to such a thing when he had the security of his sturdy flying machine. During the war, hundreds of balloonists acting as artillery spotters and observers had their balloons shot down and saved themselves by parachute. Parachutes were okay for balloons and observers, but no respectable pilot would be caught dead with one—and sure enough, none were.

When the chivalry of the aviation fraternity fell apart and enemy pilots began shooting at each other instead of waving, some great pilots died because they were without chutes. Some apparently considered it cowardly to wear a parachute, feeling that bailing out of a plane was dishonorable. The German pilots didn't think so and began wearing static-line-operated Heineke sack-type parachutes, similar to those used in jumping from balloons. In 1916 an Austrian pilot on the Russian front successfully bailed out after his plane was shot to rags. A few weeks later another Austrian pilot saved his life by bailing out. From that time on, all German and Austrian pilots wore parachutes. The British, French, and Americans were still reluctant to use a parachute and many leaped from flaming planes, preferring to die in the fatal plunge than burn in the falling wreckage. Just as the war ended, a few Allied pilots began to carry parachutes in their planes.

The war had stimulated aviation more in those few years than all the aeronautical geniuses of the world had been able to do since the dawn of history. The successful use of the parachute during the last stages of the war convinced the United States government that a reliable parachute needed to be developed.

In 1918, a board was set up by the U.S. government to begin development of a parachute that would meet the following requirements:

1. It must be possible for the aviator to leave the aircraft regardless of the position it might be in when disabled.
2. The operating means must not depend on the aviator falling from the aircraft [as the static-line-operated parachutes did].
3. The parachute equipment must be fastened to the body of the aviator at all times while he is in the aircraft [the chute was stowed in a bag in the plane and a strap with hook was fastened to the jumper, who pulled the chute after him as he fell].
4. The operating means must not be complicated or liable to foul, and it must not be susceptible to damage through any ordinary service conditions.
5. The parachute must be of such size and so disposed as to give maximum comfort to the wearer and permit him to leave the aircraft with the least difficulty or delay.
6. The parachute must open promptly and must be capable of withstanding the shock incurred by a 200-pound load falling at a speed of 300 miles per hour.
7. The parachute must be steerable to a reasonable degree.
8. The harness must be comfortable and very strong and designed so as to transfer the shock of opening in such a manner as to prevent physical injury to the aviator. It must also be sufficiently adjustable to fit the largest and smallest person.
9. The harness must be so designed that it will prevent the aviator from falling out when the parachute opens, regardless of his position in the air, and at the same time it must be possible to remove the harness when landing in the water or in a high wind.
10. The strength "follow through" must be uniform from the harness to the top of the parachute—bearing in mind the old axiom—"No chain is stronger than its weakest link."
11. The parachute must be so designed that it is easily repacked with little time and labor.

All these conditions sound fairly rigid even by today's standards. Remember, though, these conditions were being made when only a static-type parachute was in use and then usually from a balloon or slow-moving airplane.

The board included such men as Major E. L. Hoffman, Guy M. Ball, Ralph Bottriel, J. J. Higgins, Floyd Smith, and J. M. Russell. They tested every known parachute of that time, foreign and domestic, and none would qualify. Leo Stevens and Glenn Martin had worked earlier with Charles 'Broadwick in developing an attached-type parachute that could be worn by the jumper and activated by a static line. Stevens had actually suggested a free-fall type parachute which would be manually operated, as early as 1908. Most parachutes, however, had remained in a sack attached to the balloon or plane. The jumper fell away with nothing but a belt hooked to a strap leading up to the suspension lines.

Only a parachute that could be worn on the jumper and activated manually at a safe distance from the disabled plane could be accepted. Static lines and sack-type deployments would easily tangle with the falling craft and drag the parachutist down with it.

There was one big catch to a free-fall type parachute: almost everybody still believed that the air would be sucked from the jumper's body as he fell and he would be unconscious or dead within seconds. Pilots may have fabricated this myth during the war to comfort themselves after seeing a fellow aviator leap to his death to escape a flaming plane.

Leslie "Sky-Hi" Irvin didn't believe this. As a parachutist he had dropped more than two hundred times using the static-line arrangement from balloons and planes and had never felt a loss of breath during the brief plunge before the chute completely inflated. He had also performed in a circus, high-diving 80 feet into a net, with no difficulty breathing. These two reasons were enough to convince him that he would not die simply from falling free of the plane. There was still another reason he didn't believe the unconsciousness theory. During his earlier parachuting days, he saw a parachutist fall to his death. Irvin was standing only yards away from the point of fatal impact and had seen the man flailing his arms and legs right to the moment of contact. "Sky-Hi" reasoned that, if a man can wave his arms and legs all the way to the ground, he must be conscious and therefore able to activate a parachute. Irvin may have been the first to conclude that it isn't the fall that hurts, it's the sudden stop.

Yet there was still another problem. Many people still felt that a person in space, even if conscious, would be little more than a helpless glob, unable to effectively control his movements without a firm footing for leverage. Based on his own body control during high dives into the net, Irvin was convinced he could maintain control of his movements as well as remain conscious. To prove it, he volunteered to make the world's first free-fall jump.

Sixty years before Chris Wentzel took this photo of Carl Boenish and friends flying at 8,000 feet, free fall was thought to be suicide. It was believed a person would be unable to breathe, air would be sucked from his lungs, and unconsciousness and death would result. Even if he could remain conscious, they said, with nothing to brace against, movement would be impossible. (Carl Boenish)

On April 28, 1919, Leslie Irvin buckled on the model A, manually operated parachute and climbed into a De Havilland DH-9 biplane at McCook Field near Dayton, Ohio. At the controls was Floyd Smith. In telling of this dramatic moment in his life, Irvin said it wasn't until he stood up in the cockpit, 1,500 feet over McCook Field, that he found himself rapidly losing confidence in his ability to stay conscious, control his movements, and activate the parachute. He didn't hesitate any longer, but dived headfirst over the side, delayed only a few seconds, then easily pulled the ripcord with both hands. The parachute blossomed perfectly and an exuberant Irvin descended. Although he broke his ankle when he struck the ground, he said he smiled all the way to the hospital!

He had reason to smile. Not only was he still alive, but he had proved—or disproved—several points about free-falling bodies. He demonstrated that it is possible for a man falling through space to remain conscious, think, and make coordinated movements to release a parachute manually.

Irvin was one of our earliest test jumpers. Although making a jump-and-pull hardly sounds daring to the present-day sport jumper, it was extremely so in Irvin's day—or at least everybody thought so. He faced the same enemy in 1919 that humans have faced since the dawn of time and still face today—the un-

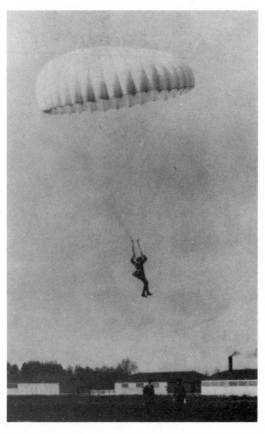

Leslie L. Irvin descends on McCook Field near Dayton, Ohio, in 1919 after making the first free-fall parachute jump in history. (Irving Air Chute Co.)

known. Our instinctive fear of the unknown is as basic as our instinctive fear of falling—and the test jumper must overcome both. The parachuting world lost a great man when Irvin passed away in 1966.

During the 1920's, aviation boomed. Irvin built a parachute factory and his parachutes saw plenty of action. While Major Hoffman's group began working on the next great problem—delayed free fall—flying circuses barnstormed the country. Surplus airplanes from World War I were easy to buy—still "in the manufacturer's container," as we say today. Men like Charles A. Lindbergh and James H. Doolittle bought their planes in a box, assembled them on the spot, and flew them away. Some flew away to fame and fortune, some just flew away, and some never got off the ground.

After barnstorming the country, first as a parachutist and then as a flyer, Lindbergh took up flying the mail. And although he had saved his life by parachute four times—twice in the military, twice flying the mail—he made his historic Atlantic flight without one. Jimmy Doolittle also saved himself with a parachute on four separate occasions. His fourth jump was at night over China after his historic B-25 raid on Tokyo. Others on that mission bailed out—one died jumping, several were killed or captured by the Japanese, and the rest made it back to become heroes. One accidentally opened his chute in the plane, re-packed it, finished just as the engine ran out of fuel, and then safely bailed out!

In 1922 Lieutenant Harold R. Harris (who retired as a general) made the first emergency jump from a disabled plane and saved his life with an Air Ser-vice parachute. Less than a month later Lieutenant Frank Tyndall became the second man to jump from a disabled plane and save his life with the type of parachute developed by the Air Service Board. Shortly after this, several people suggested forming some sort of club for those who saved their lives by para-chute, and the Caterpillar Club was born. Harris and Tyndall, both military pilots, became the first two members, although earlier William O'Connor had saved himself with a chest reserve when his Jahn chute failed.

The list of names from the Roster of the Caterpillar Club, faithfully main-tained by the Irvin organization, reads like a *Who's Who in Aviation*. By 1935 the club had a membership of more than a thousand grateful airmen . . . and air-women like Mrs. Irene McFarland. She saved her life over Cincinnati on July 4, 1925—a month after Lindbergh's second emergency jump. By the end of World War II, parachutes had saved more than 80,000 lives. Thrilling stories of many of these jumps are related in Ian Mackersey's book, *Into the Silk*.

During the 1920's, planes were continuously being improved to go higher and faster. High-speed emergency bailouts were inevitable and the parachute test section went to work on the problems of delayed free fall. The delayed fall was necessary to allow the pilot's body to slow down for the parachute opening. Men like Randall Bose and Steven Budreau bailed out at altitudes of up to 7,000 feet to experience the first encounters with the deadly flat spin.

From tests, it was discovered that the free-falling human body accelerates up to 120 mph and then, in a flat position, falls no faster. This speed is referred to as "terminal velocity" and might be compared to the sonic barrier for airplanes. Terminal velocity is reached in approximately twelve seconds, after the drop of roughly 1,500 feet. The test jumpers experienced very little difficulty up to ter-minal velocity, but delays past 1,500 feet brought on various peculiar forces, especially the tendency to rotate. This turning would be relatively slow at first and, depending on the movement of the body, would rapidly accelerate until everything became a blur or it would stop and counterrotate. There seemed to be a constant battle to maintain a heading. More jumpers like Crawford, Mor-gan, and Whitby made delays, sometimes fighting off the spin, sometimes resort-ing to the ripcord before losing consciousness. Free-fall testing reached a climax in August 1960, when Captain Joseph W. Kittinger stepped into space at 102,800 feet. He had fallen sixteen seconds and reached a speed of 614 mph in the rarified air when a six-foot stabilizing chute automatically deployed to pre-

Early jumpers took their chances in rickety airplanes as well as in homemade parachutes made of cotton sheets and clothesline. This is Jack Clapp with his parachute just before an exhibition jump.

vent spinning during the next four and a half minutes of fall before his main chute automatically opened. He tells his story in his book, *The Long, Lonely Leap*.

While the military test parachute group was cautiously and scientifically tackling the problems of delayed free fall from 8,000 feet, civilians like Art Starnes and Spud Manning were making exhibition delays from as high as 18,000 feet.

The barnstormers and their flying circuses were in the public eye. Scientific test jumpers were not. As a result, the parachute kept its image as a stuntman's gimmick—just as in the days of balloons. To the general public, the parachute was strictly for daredevils who liked to flirt with death or for aviators who had no choice. Unfortunately, this same general feeling exists even today.

Parachute jumps were a necessary part of any airshow, as much as the airplane itself, but because people could watch the show from the surrounding countryside, the air circus people had to get down near the ground and put on some stunts that only the paying customer could see—those right at the field, not half a mile away. This is when the performers began doing head-on automobile collisions, car-to-plane transfers, and wingwalking. Art Starnes had a leather pad sewn in his thick canvas pants and would drop from a plane a few feet off the ground, scooting along in a cloud of dust with his famous seat-of-the-pants death-defying slide. Everybody within miles could see his parachute jump, but only the paying customers saw that "slide of death" act. Somehow, though, the parachute was associated with the same absurd stunt.

Another parachutist, Buddy (Emmett L.) Plunkett, should have had Art's leather-bottomed pants for a stunt he did at Daytona Beach. He was making a car-to-plane transfer. Standing on a roadster and facing backward as it roared down the beach, he waited for the Jenny to overtake them. The first pass was too fast and Plunkett signaled the pilot to slow down. The second pass was slow enough but too high and he missed it. The pilot thought he was still too fast so slowed down even more for the third pass. Plunkett had no difficulty grabbing a wing-skid and swinging his legs up around it. His weight on the wingtip plus the slow airspeed caused the plane to dip, then skim along the sand with Plunkett hanging on for dear life. He bounced along, seat first, a la Starnes, but sans padding. After his rear had been sanded sufficiently, it was treated to a "soothing" saltwater bath as the pilot turned out to sea in an effort to gain altitude.

Barnstormers mixed wingwalking and ground-to-air transfers with the parachuting and stunt flying—giving parachuting the daredevil connotation it still has. Here Buddy Plunkett reenacts some of his wingwalking routine.

In the late 1920's Emmett L. "Buddy" Plunkett thrilled thousands with his barnstorming acts. He survived to become a colonel in the Air Force. Colonel Plunkett owned and operated a certified parachute loft near Atlanta, Georgia. He died in 1971.

Plunkett still hung on for dear life, his raw rear slapping the tops off waves as he went.

Starting out as a wingwalker for Mabel Cody's Flying Circus in Atlanta, the fourteen-year-old Plunkett immediately took to parachutes and thrilled crowds all over the southeastern states with his daring stunts both with and without a parachute. He became known for his long delayed free falls—one from 23,000 down to 9,000 feet—and repeated "malfunctions." Actually he carried an old torn chute, let it trail a few thousand feet, and would then open his main. Without a doubt, his most spectacular and death-defying parachute jump came over Tampa Bay when he soaked his plane with gasoline and ignited it! He secured a can of gasoline to the top wing of the old biplane and then ran copper tubing down and out along the leading edges of the port and starboard lower wings to each wingtip. He put a valve under the can and punched holes in the copper tubing. On each wingtip he installed a spark plug, wired to a booster magneto in the cockpit. The idea was to release the gasoline along the wings, ignite it, and as the plane was slowly consumed by flames, bail out. It worked pretty well up to the point where he released his seat belt and cranked the magneto. Apparently the gasoline had not just trickled back along the lower

By the time the CAA came into being and issued a ruling that required exhibition parachutists to wear two parachutes, Buddy Plunkett already had over a hundred jumps with only one. Here he proudly displays his dual rig.

wing but had been picked up in the propblast and whipped up onto the bottom of the upper wing and the sides of the fuselage, too. When the spark ignited the gasoline, the entire plane exploded into flames instantly. Plunkett dived over the side and delayed his opening long enough to watch the plane arch over in a ball of flames and dive toward the Gulf of Mexico. He opened his chute and settled gently into Tampa Bay, where a boat was waiting and recovered him. The nineteen-year-old collected a nifty $1,200 for the stunt.

During the 1930's parachuting saw another gimmick come into play—bat wings. Even today the bat wings are used occasionally. Outlawed by The United States Parachute Association, bat wings have seldom been used for much more than display purposes. The typical bat-winged jumper would walk around in front of the crowd, swooping his canvas and stick contraption up and down, demonstrating how he would be using it in flight. It made a good show on the ground—and still does, for that matter—the crowds loved it. But in the air, that's a horse of another color. With few exceptions, the bat-winged parachutist would plummet like a crated piano, usually trailing a sack of flour to mark his trail as he fell.

Clem Sohn was killed in Vincennes, France, on April 25, 1937, when his

Bat wings are more valuable for showmanship on the ground than gliding through the air. Pictured here are Tommy Boyd, Don Molitar, and Lyle Cameron. (**Sky Diver** Magazine)

parachute fouled in the bat wings. He had successfully demonstrated his wings a couple of times in Miami. One account reported that, "Leaping from a plane only 3,000 feet up over Portsmouth Airport, Hants, England, Clem Sohn swooped like a bird for a mile, then parachuted into a tree." He wore a standard backpack and used a seatpack for an emergency chute, leaving his chest free of obstructions for a better glide. His bat wings consisted of treated canvas over metal rods strapped to his arms, waist, and legs, and another piece of canvas fixed between his legs. His last jump was from 10,000 feet and he supposedly glided down to within 700 feet of the ground before pulling his main. The pilot chute caught in a wing, preventing the canopy from inflating. He then pulled his reserve seatpack at 250 feet, but it fouled in the other malfunction and he was killed on impact.

Another 1937 report tells of Manos Morgan, who started his jump from 10,000 feet and glided for 90 seconds before opening his parachute at 1,400 feet, landing safely. Without wings, he would have covered the distance in 53 seconds. His wings were three and a half feet across and were made of steel tubing with airplane fabric.

Tommy Boyd wore a seatpack for his reserve when using bat wings. Unlike Sohn, Boyd was still alive at last accounting and his glide was said to approach 30 to 40 degrees (45 degrees is considered tops in maximum track without wings). Tommy filled his leg fin with red powder and pinned it shut with clothespins. When he jumped, a static line pulled the pins, allowing him to trail the dust down to the opening at four or five hundred feet. This low opening might account for the optimum glide ratio since the lower the opening, the greater the illusion of distance traveled.

Although his wings apparently had nothing to do with it, Rudolf Boehlen of Switzerland died of internal bleeding the day after three successful flights. He is thought to have struck his head during a backward parachute landing fall.

Probably the best known of the winged jumpers was Leo Valentin. He died with his wings on in 1956 when the propblast from his jump plane smashed one wing against the door and he hurtled to his death. Valentin deserves special credit, although he ended up just as dead as the others. He was the first to perfect delayed free-fall techniques. He dreamed of someday accomplishing flight without using the parachute—actually landing with his wings. He had several close calls in his career with various types of nonrigid wings and, after a particularly harrowing experience in 1950, concluded that this type of wing could do little more than slow the free fall. It became obvious to him, he said, that it was impossible to glide with nonrigid wings.

He designed a set of rigid wings some 9 feet long with a hinged arrangement on a steel tube corset for his chest. As he was about to test the 28-pound rig from a helicopter, "I have rarely felt so hideously insecure," he later stated. Leo was a master of understatement. The wings were stressed to lock up against a support so they could be folded forward but not back; this was necessary to keep the wings from folding behind him and breaking both arms. He was right: it worked perfectly as he began his drop from 4,000 feet. Suddenly he was flipped on his back, the wings closed back together with a slam—and he began the horrible, panic-stricken ride down, spinning on his back, struggling to free his arm of the wings so he could pull the ripcord. He never figured how he did it, but the ripcord was pulled at 900 feet. He lowered his corset and wings to the ground on a rigging line. His friends and fellow batmen, Salvador Canarrozzo and Soro Rinaldi, congratulated him for surviving. Salvador, who developed the arrowlike inverted "Y" position of stable free fall, was to die in 1953 when his one and only chute failed at 450 feet.

In his book *Bird Man*, Valentin tells of watching his two friends perform. After watching these bat-winged companions jump with flapping canvas wings, Valentin realized he needed more than mere surface if he were to glide successfully. He designed rigid wings with a true airfoil and took flying lessons to better understand the art of flying and gliding.

Valentin's final set of wings were of balsa wood, weighed 28 pounds, and had a locking system that, once they opened, held them open with no danger of collapse. He had tested his "tail"—canvas stretched between the legs in one large solid section—and discovered it caused spinning, so this was eliminated. After testing his new wooden wings in a wind tunnel—first on a dummy and then on himself—he made his first jump with them on May 9, 1954, becoming the first birdman to truly fly, covering more than three miles from 9,000 feet on the first attempt.

Because Valentin made his living as a professional parachutist, he was billed as "Valentin, the Most Daring Man in the World." He had no objection to this billing, since it produced his living, but he said it was only a constant warning to him to practice prudence at all times. He found himself making a jump with canvas wings in order to fulfill a contract, but observed, ". . . it was painful for me to be forced, in order to satisfy a press and public more eager for sensations than for quality and research, to go on with a stunt which I knew led nowhere." Leo kept carefully within the safety limits (1,000 feet for the opening is France's safety limit—six seconds above the ground) and shuddered at the recklessness of his fellow birdmen. He said he was neither a madman nor an eccentric. To him, parachuting was a serious business and he carefully packed his chutes, carefully checked his instruments, always opened within safe limits. He was not the first to point out that the risk is great enough when a pure accident is still possible. Valentin was highly critical of Salvador Canarrozzo, whom he called both a wonderful pal and a most daring parachutist. Canarrozzo always jumped without helmet, goggles, watch or altimeter, or a reserve parachute. He would judge his own time for pulling the ripcord, usually no higher than 500 feet ("When a Ford looks like a Ford," as my good friend Johnny Findley likes to put it). The reckless Italian birdman made his last impression at Venice in April 1953. The safety-conscious, careful, prudent Valentin died in May, three years later.

A safe and useful descendent of the sticks-and-canvas bat wing is today's nonrigid extensions. This is simply excess material built into the jumpsuit between the waist and elbow that increases drag when the elbow is extended. The effect is similar to that of the excess skin on a flying squirrel. Today's free-fall photographers' jumpsuits have such extensions to furnish a stable platform from which to film as well as to regulate the rate of descent and horizontal movement.

While exhibitionists were wingwalking, making midair plane transfers, or otherwise displaying more guts than skill, pilots were competing in air races. It was traditional at air races to supplement the show with a demonstration parachute jump or two. A fee of $100 or so would be paid the jumper and that would pretty much be the end of that until the next year's races. Sometimes the jumper would land in front of the people and sometimes he would float halfway to Timbuktu—these were nonsteerable parachutes. Steerable sport parachutes were still twenty years away. To get a top-notch jumper who could always land at least on the airport (don't laugh), the fee would be higher—up to $500 for some jumpers.

One jumper back in 1926 suggested to the Pulitzer Races authorities that instead of hiring one man to jump at their Philadelphia show, why not put the money up as a prize and invite several jumpers to compete for it? This way the show would get more jumpers, better jumpers, and still pay no more than for one. The idea sounded good to jumpers and sponsors alike and the jumper who had suggested it, Joe Crane, became the father of competition jumping. This wasn't sport, though—that's for glory—this was strictly professional, winner take all. A circle was made on the field and the jumper whose average was closest to this spot walked off with a cash prize. The others walked off with experience. This "spot jumping" contest became a popular event in future airshows and at the National Air Races.

The race was held annually and the number of jumpers increased each year. By 1932, 46 contestants signed up to compete. Up to then, the jumps were unsupervised and every man was independent of all factors except himself. Crane was placed in complete charge of the jumpers during the two-day air meet at Roosevelt Field in the fall of 1932. He organized the group and scheduled the jumps so that instead of having the confusion of previous races, the jump program came off smoothly, each jumper knowing exactly what he was to do. Although jumping had been secondary to the air races, it began to have a place of its own now. The National Aeronautics Association had not been interested in the jumpers but only in the pilots. However, NAA's Bill Enyart recognized parachuting as a vital drawing card for the races and formed a parachute committee with Joe Crane as president. A few months later a group of professional jumpers met at Roosevelt Field and formed the National Parachute Jumpers Association. The organization set minimum charges for air meets. During the Thirties, Crane maintained records and sent out periodic newsletters to the more than a hundred members. By the time World War II broke out, NPJA had 250 members. Although continuing to work closely with NAA at the air races, Crane and his jumpers' association maintained their independence.

During this same period—the late 1920's and early 1930's—a Russian military attaché visiting the United States was impressed with the parachuting practices of the Americans. He and his military leaders realized the potential military advantage of trained parachutists and took the idea back to Russia in 1925. Stalin himself ordered jump schools to train boys and girls as well as adults. The next year, the American parachutist Lyman Ford made the first free-fall parachute jump ever made in Russia. (Thirty years later, as president of Pioneer Parachute Company, Ford furnished the first U.S. parachute team with the chutes they used in Moscow during the Third World Parachuting Championships.) In 1927 the Russians demonstrated how nine paratroopers could parachute behind the lines and dynamite enemy installations. By 1932, trained military parachutists had reached a degree of proficiency that enabled them, during war games, to capture the entire "enemy" headquarters and all the Soviet officers in command of the opposing force.

The parachute first turned up for sport jumping in 1930, when the Russians held a special sport festival that included a spot jumping contest. These were not professionals jumping for money, but civilian factory workers jumping for nothing more than fun and honors. In 1933, the year after NAA created a parachuting committee in the United States, the Soviet government grouped all Russian parachute clubs under one national organization.

With the government supporting the movement, sport parachuting engulfed Russia. By the mid-1930's Russia was making mass drops of 5,700 military troops and had begun dropping light tanks and artillery pieces. The Russian troops used automatic openers rather than static lines. In 1935, sport jumpers were training on 559 state-subsidized training towers at the 115 parachute centers. These same sport jumpers needed only military training to become expert paratroopers. By 1939, they became parachutists fighting in the Russo-Finnish wars—and winnning.

While sport parachuting can be credited to the Russians in 1930 (regardless of their motive), seeing the military application of the parachute goes back to an American, Benjamin Franklin, who suggested the idea in 1784. In 1928 Billy Mitchell arranged for six soldiers to parachute from a bomber over Kelly Field, assemble a machine gun, and set up a defensive position in a matter of only minutes. He had suggested the idea ten years earlier during World War I. The ranking officers who witnessed the demonstration of airborne mobility and firepower enjoyed the show but failed to be impressed with the military significance. It wasn't until 1940 that William Ryder and William Lee led the original 48 volunteers through training to become the first American paratroopers.

Both the Germans and French had been impressed by the Russian paratroop exercises and both began to train their own military jumpers. The French, like the Russians, used free-fall parachutes. Unlike the Russians, the French allowed each man to pull his ripcord rather than having it pulled by an automatic opener. This meant that some opened their chutes immediately on exit and a few didn't open at all—the rest were straggled out in between, at the mercy of the winds and the sharpshooters below. This could account for the French more or less giving up their parachute troops but becoming the leaders in the art of delayed free fall.

The Germans carefully weighed the evidence of the Russians and the French and developed the static line which put all troops open at the same altitude and kept them in one group rather than scattered all over the sky and countryside. In 1936 Raymond Quilter presented a static-line system for military troops, but the British War Office wasn't interested. The British, like the Americans, failed to see any real significance in parachute troops until *after* World War II broke out.

Then in 1940 the Germans dropped storm troopers on Holland and took the city of Rotterdam entirely with airborne troops. The British and Americans suddenly saw the light and both immediately initiated crash programs. There was little reason why those German troop carriers couldn't have flown another few minutes and dumped German troops on Great Britain instead of Holland. That 20-mile moat no longer gave the British the sense of security.

The weather in Great Britain often leaves much to be desired when it comes to flying or parachuting, so part of the training was done indoors. Moored balloons inside huge hangars were used as training towers. The jumper was released with his canopy already held open, just as with American jump towers. Night and day, rain or shine, training continued on a crash basis. After the indoor training, the British paratrooper made seven jumps—two from a moored balloon and five from an airplane—to receive his jump wings.

In the early days of parachute troop training, only the Americans and Russians wore reserves. Consequently, fatalities among the French, German, and British troops were more frequent. During early training, a fatal accident was considered a good thing as long as it happened to somebody else—the rest of the troops felt another fatal accident immediately after the first was unlikely and for the next few days the air would remain safe.

While Russian and Germany were using the parachute as a military weapon against their fellowman, in the United States the Government Forest Service began to train parachute troops to fight fires. The idea had been tried in 1934 by J. B. Bruce, but it was abandoned as too risky and efforts were concentrated on chemical bombing of fires. By 1939 it became obvious that the available planes could not do the job and Frank M. Derry was put in charge of a group of professional jumpers who would parachute in to fight fires. Early results showed that in only nine fires, the men had saved three times the cost of the entire project, earning a permanent slot in parachuting history. Over the past 25 years, smoke jumpers have proved themselves to be invaluable, saving millions of dollars worth of valuable forests.

World War II saw the parachute expand in several fields—especially airborne troops and aerial delivery of military equipment—but the most outstanding and exciting stories come from the emergency uses: airmen leaping for their lives. More than 100,000 persons saved their lives with parachutes during that war. Some, like British pilot Tony Woods-Scawen, saved themselves several times. Woods-Scawen was shot down five times, safely parachuting to earth

(Above left) The Barish Sailwing, introduced in late 1965, is ancestor of a number of designs that have reached the sport parachuting market. Although it produced the outstanding forward speed desirable, opening shock and opening reliability presented problems. Dependent on forward speed for its lift, it stalled like an airplane at slow speeds and dropped like a rock. (Jerry Irwin)

(Above right) Irvin Industries and Steve Snyder pooled efforts to come up with the Delta II Parawing. The slotted wing and improved deployment system put this design out in front of the solid delta-wing designs and was an ancestor of the Pterodactyl. (U.S. Navy)

(Left) Astronaut Ed White's 21-minute space walk ranks among the longest "free falls" on record. But Bill Dause of Pope Valley, California, had more than 60 hours in free fall when he received USPA's 7,000-jump certificate in November 1979. Both the astronaut and the skydiver experience similar sensations of weightlessness, but unlike the free-falling jumper, who uses the air to turn and maneuver his body, White used a hand-held, self-maneuvering unit. (NASA)

(Above left) Pioneer's Para-Commander revolutionized sport jumping in 1964. Although many others offered "plus" features, the PC became the most common and widely accepted (and copied) sport parachute in the entire world. (U.S. Navy)

(Above right) Para-Flite's high-performance emergency parachute, the *Safety-Flyer*™ pictured here, saves you in sheer luxury. This square canopy is much more reliable in opening than the old round reserves, yet lets you down more softly with complete maneuverability. (Para-Flite Inc.)

(Right) In 1970 the ram-air parachutes came on the scene. By the end of the decade they had been perfected and became the overwhelming choice of all experienced jumpers. This flexible glider is constructed with cells, which when ram-air inflated, create a pressurized semi-rigid wing with upper and lower surfaces and an airfoil section. A pioneer in the development of the ram-air canopy, Steve Snyder is responsible for a number of excellent designs such as this one from Para-Flite. (Para-Flite Inc.)

the first four; the fifth escape was too low for the parachute to deploy and he was killed.

Others survived to greater glories. Colonel Charles E. Yeager is a good example. Early in his flying career the engine of his Bell Airacobra blew up and his cockpit filled with flames. The P-39 went into a power dive and Yeager fought the flames and his safety harness at the same time. He fought his way clear, tumbling first, then gyrating wildly on his back as he pulled the ripcord. The high-speed opening shock knocked him unconscious. He woke up in a hospital, where doctors told him he would fly again—and did he ever!

Late in 1944, the day after he had shot down a German Me-109, a swarm of FW-190's raked his Mustang with cannon shells. The engine and oxygen system exploded into flames and his well-ventilated cockpit became a raging furnace. With shell fragments in his feet and a badly cut arm, Yeager dived into space 20,000 feet over enemy territory. To avoid hanging like a clay pigeon for the twenty minutes of descent, he delayed his opening for more than a minute, opening his parachute at 5,000 feet. Although enemy troops were all around him and he could hardly walk because of his wounds, he avoided capture and made his way back to England.

Those of us who know him can hardly imagine him ever being angry, but Chuck Yeager didn't like walking home and he got downright mad. His first mission out he shot down a German bomber. On a mission a few days later, he shot down five German fighters, and a few weeks later his propeller-driven Mustang shot down a new Messerschmitt Me-262 *jet* fighter. Two weeks later he blasted four more German fighters out of the sky. In a matter of a few months the mild-mannered, quiet-talking West Virginian had twelve confirmed air-to-air kills. Yet today Yeager is best known as the first man to fly faster than the speed of sound, pushing the old Bell XS-1 through the barrier in 1947. He hit 760.5 mph in level flight, then a few years later he more than doubled that speed to again set a world's record. He insists that it took no courage for him to bail out of his plane either time—that jumping out was so much better than staying inside, he probably would have done it without a parachute.

Thousands of exciting stories came from parachuting episodes during the war and many good books are filled with stranger-than-fiction accounts.

After the war, some of the returning military parachutists continued making jumps as civilians, just for fun. Some attempted long delays, panicked, and pulled the reserve instead of the main. Sometimes the rig was unsafe and the reserve would rip off on opening. Unfamiliar with the free-fall pack, the ex-paratrooper would fall to his death without attempting to open his main parachute. The Civil Aeronautics Board issued a regulation outlawing delayed free falls at airshows, but Joe Crane's NPJA expanded to take in certified riggers and became National Parachute Jumpers-Riggers, Inc., NPJR. Crane worked through the NAA to establish parachute records with the Federation Aeronautique Internationale. In 1948, the FAI set up an international parachuting commission and the NPJR affiliated with NAA. The commission set up rules for records and competitions, paving the way for the First World Parachuting Championship, which was held in Yugoslavia in 1951. No Americans took part in the first championships; there were representatives from only five countries and the winner was Pierre Lard of France. When France hosted the Second World Parachuting Championship in 1954, the number of nations had increased to eight and Sergeant Fred Mason, competing as the only U.S. entry, finished twenty-first. The Russians won the event and so became host in Moscow in 1956. Between 1954 and 1956, NPJR members expressed some concern that the Americans had only one contestant rather than a team—Fred Mason looked pretty lonesome in those pictures that showed complete men and women teams for several countries.

One such concerned person was Jacques Istel, who vowed to do something about it. He was a delegate in 1955 to the Commission of International Parachuting Championship. While in Europe, he took time off in his native France (Istel is a naturalized American), where Sam Chasak and Michel Prik taught him the basics of controlled free fall. Istel came back and immediately went to work promoting an American team. He worked with the late Joe Crane and the NPJR, sent out invitations, and trained those who could participate. In 1956 he led the first American team into world parachuting competition. From then on, the U.S. team grew in size and prestige, with Americans either winning or placing in the top positions.

When Istel began pushing the sport in 1956, interest began to grow among people other than professional jumpers or ex-paratroopers. College groups got together the next year for an intercollegiate meet and clubs began to spring up across the country. By late 1957 the NPJR had changed its name once more and became the Parachute Club of America, again with Joe Crane as president. The next year, Jacques Istel and Lewis B. Sanborn set up Parachutes Incorporated and devoted full time to sport parachute promotion. Shortly afterward, they opened the first commercial sport parachuting centers at Orange, Massachusetts, and at Hemet, California. In 1967, the Parachute Club of America became the United States Parachute Association, with Norman Heaton remaining as executive director.

The late Joe Crane deserves a position of honor for giving birth to competition jumping and for keeping parachuting alive and organized for the first thirty years. Jacques Istel can be credited with giving birth to skydiving techniques and true sport parachuting in America.

Those of us who started out with nonsteerable, flat circular chutes like to think those were the "good old days" when it took a real man to make a delayed free fall. When the ripcord was pulled, you closed your eyes, gritted your teeth, and yanked. After the stars cleared and vision returned once more, you'd check to see how much canopy had been blown away—those holes weren't modifications then, they were honest-to-goodness holes! A few holes were good for cutting down the miserable seesaw oscillation that would rock you into urpy nausea. Then came the fun of trying to guess where you were going to land.

British jumper Dumbo Willans said it and maybe we should call it Willans' Law: "There seems to be some kind of natural law by which parachutes generally avoid the really disastrous obstructions while taking every opportunity to land their 'pilots' in undignified and uncomfortable situations—sewage dumps, chicken farms, guard-dog compounds, grape arbours, tall trees, and church spires." I look back on those days of jumping in the same vein as my military experience—I wouldn't take a million dollars for the experience, but I wouldn't want to go through it again, either.

The sleeve for more positive and more gentle openings and the truly steerable canopies had a great deal to do with the growth of the sport and the reduction of injuries and fatalities. Istel introduced them both to popular usage in the United States. His limitless energy and personal drive pulled parachuting out of its doldrums and changed the attitude of many anti-parachuting officials.

The military, which had made free-fall parachuting a court-martial offense, reversed its decision and retained Istel to train a select group of military men in the art of free-fall parachuting. These seven men became the cadre of instructors for the Army. Early in 1958, AR 95-19 authorized army personnel to compete and take part in delayed free-fall parachuting. The other military branches later issued similar regulations. Istel had cracked the toughest opposition and turned the tide in his favor. He gave talks and demonstrations to state aviation officials who at first were anti-parachuting. The result was that those of us who were outlaw-jumping in defiance of state laws could at last jump with state approval. Moreover, state approval opened the way for the formation of parachute clubs at various airports and invitations could be extended to interested spectators.

Convincing state officials of the safety of parachuting—when properly conducted—was one thing. Convincing the federal government was something else, though. In 1961 Istel had not only convinced the Federal Aviation Agency that parachuting should be recognized, he talked the FAA administrator, Najeeb Halaby, into making a sport jump at the Orange Sport Parachute Center. For good measure, Crocker Snow of the Massachusetts Aeronautics Commission came along and jumped, too. Talk about selling refrigerators to Eskimos . . .

In the fall of 1961, NAA asked FAI to send a list of the current world records on parachuting. Of the 82 world records, every one was held by an Iron Curtain country; Russia alone held 60 of them! Immediately, Istel and Sanborn, with two of their parachute center's instructors, Nate Pond and Bill Jolly, went to work to beat the Russians. In November 1961 they broke the old Russian records and set new ones in the four-man team night-and-day group accuracy with delayed-opening category—the first of many U.S. entries in world parachuting records. By January 1962 there were 124 world records on file with the FAI. The two U.S. records and one new French record represented the entire free world. Later, in 1962, the United States began an all-out effort to capture more records. Within two years, the U.S. Army Parachute Team held 70 of them.

Meanwhile, the United States continued to enter parachute teams at the World Parachuting Championships. The United States had come in sixth out of ten in its first attempt in 1956; then, in 1958, in Czechoslovakia, it again placed sixth—but this time out of fourteen. In 1960, in Bulgaria, Barbara Gray and Sherrie Buck represented the women jumpers of America for the first time, but only as individuals, since four were required to make a team. At this, the Fifth World Parachuting Championship, the U.S. team placed fourth overall, but Jim Arender became the individual world style champion and Dick Fortenberry placed second overall, having scored the first dead-center ever recorded in world championship competition. We were on the move now and hosted the 1962 event at Orange, Massachusetts. This was the largest so far, consisting of 26 countries and 136 individual contestants. But on our home field we did the best yet. Jim Arender and Muriel Simbro took the overall World Champion title for men and women. Our men's team placed second to the Czechoslovakian team, but our women took first place. We repeated the performance in the 1964 world meet in West Germany when Dick Fortenberry and Tee Taylor took overall champion titles and our women won first place. The men's team dropped to third behind Czechoslovakia and Russia. The Eighth (1966) World Championships were scheduled for East Germany—a country not recognized by many of the Western nations. As a result, the United States and several other nations did not take part. Since only six nations are required for the World Championship, the game went on without us. For locations and results of succeeding World Championships, see the Appendix. For more comprehensive coverage of competitions in both national and world meets, refer to Chapter 6.

We've covered a lot of ground—or should we say air—since Leonardo doodled his "tent" design. Special parachutes have been developed that range in size from a foot or so up to one hundred feet or more. The uses are endless—some will be discussed at length later in the book. Most developments in parachutes, like in aircraft, have come within the twentieth century. Special caliber men have risked their lives in developing the parachute and the related escape systems. From towers, balloons, and airplanes, for money, life, and honor, the parachutist today has a rich and exciting heritage.

2. The Panic Button!

Emergency Jumps

Emergency parachute jumps are the ones that seem most exciting (especially to the person who makes one) and this type of parachuting is the best known to the general public.

    The average person thinks of the parachute as that one link with life after all else is gone—the panic-type, last resort, emergency situation when all else has failed and there is nothing to lose by hitting the silk. This is the reason most people think of parachuting as death-defying and dangerous. They either associate it with some unfortunate pilot whose plane is burning and breaking up in flight so bailing out means little more than *how* he'll die, not *whether* he'll die, or associate it with the barnstorming daredevil who risks life and limb flirting with death to thrill crowds and make money. The thought of bailing out of an airplane, even in an emergency, strikes terror in the average pilot. Half of the pilots you ask will tell you they would rather ride down with the plane and take

What must go down in parachuting and aviation history as that once-in-a-million event took place in March 1963 over Frejorgue, France. A parachutist named Chionni stepped from the open cockpit of a small biplane to make a routine drop. Pilot Christian de la Beaume prepared to fly back to the field and land. However, both were in for a terrifying surprise when Chionni's main parachute and harness struck the tail assembly and became hopelessly entangled. Chionni could not free himself and the plane was dragged to a stop. It then began to plunge toward earth with the pilot still in the cockpit! The pilot cut the engine, Chionni went for broke and pulled his reserve chute. Both chutes inflated properly to check the descent. Although the plane was slightly damaged and the pilot suffered a broken leg, parachutist Chionni walked away unscratched.**(Paris Match)**

their chances on the crash than bail out. The majority seem to feel their chances are better in a crash landing than in a parachute jump. There are cases that justify either choice, but survival favors the one who bails out.

An emergency jump is exactly that—an emergency. This means you have only one parachute and if it doesn't work, there's little left to do except pray . . . fast. It also means you have no choice of when, where, or how you get away from the plane. It may be at night, it may be over a city, and the plane may be tumbling end over end or spinning. These are factors that are normally eliminated in a preplanned jump such as a sport jump. For example, a sport jumper wears *two* parachutes; he chooses his own time of day and the right weather conditions; he usually jumps over open country or a prepared drop zone; and he exits a plane that is flying straight and level. Although there is little comparison between these two types of jumping, the average citizen groups them both in the same category: "a parachute jump."

Normally, when an airman encounters that panic situation and punches out, everything is a maze of blurred images and confusion. If it all works out as it should, he becomes aware of what has happened only when he is descending under the open parachute canopy. I said, "if it all works out as it should,"

Emergency jumps are made when the emergency develops, whether over trees, water, cities, or other hazardous areas. Tree landings are rare in sport jumping now. This was not so before steerable parachutes were developed. Usually the jumper drops through the tree safely while the canopy snares in the branches and arrests the fall. A greater danger lies in getting down out of the tree. If the parachutist is wearing a reserve chute, he simply leaves it attached to the harness and drops the canopy to the ground. Then he carefully slips out of the harness and slides down the reserve lines and canopy. Bud Kiesow made this tree landing for the filming of the award-winning USAF training film, *Passport to Safety*. Parachuting Associates' Dave Burt, Jim Hall, and Bob Sinclair also participated in the production. (Parachuting Associates, Inc.)

because sometimes the system fails. But when an experienced parachutist like Bob "Lizard" Waltzer was forced to eject at 17,000 feet, there was no panic for him. Instead it was an exciting new adventure, one that he could experience to its fullest. One he could savor. It was jump number 1,214.

Early in July 1979 Waltzer was a competitor in the U.S. National Parachuting Championships in Richmond, Indiana. He was competing in the 4-Way event on the High Speed Dirt team and in the 8-Way event on the Roller Ball Rules team. Between dirt dives, he and I chatted about flying and jumping. Just three weeks after our conversation in Richmond, he made his first emergency ejection over friendly Twenty-nine Palms, California.

He started the morning trying to convince the air delivery unit to let him jump with them. Although he had more than 1,200 sport jumps, they wouldn't let him participate because he wasn't military jump qualified. Before the day was over, though, he got that military jump . . . the hard way.

His flight that day would be a ground attack mission with two Marine F-4N fighter planes from his marine reserve unit. After a quick briefing, both planes took off. They were to fire their rockets on the desert target range near Twenty-nine Palms, then fly to Yuma for refueling, and continue to their home base at Andrews Air Force Base near Washington, D.C. But "the best laid schemes o' mice and men . . . ."

Captain Rick Loibl and Bob Waltzer took off first, followed by Lieutenant Colonel Fritz Menning with *Time* photographer/journalist Mark Meyer in the back seat. Meyer was going to photograph the first plane as it fired its rockets, for an article he was doing on desert warfare training. When they contacted the controller, they were instructed to orbit out of the target area until the previous flight had completed its mission and cleared the missile range. The two planes climbed to 17,000 feet, slowed to about 300 knots, and began their orbit. After about twenty minutes they still had not been cleared onto the target. Meyer was busy taking photos and signaled a thumbs up to Loibl and Waltzer, indicating that he was getting some great shots. Waltzer was computing how much fuel they had to complete the mission and make it to Yuma when it happened. Here's how Waltzer recalls it:

"All of a sudden, without any warning, there was a tremendous crash which knocked my head against the side of the canopy. A split second later I was being forced against the right side of the cockpit and realized that we were spinning upside down. I had no idea what had happened, but I looked in the rear view mirror and saw the whole back of the aircraft burning. I remember saying, 'That's good enough for me!' and reached for the lower firing handle between my legs. I could only get it with one hand, but I gave it a yank.

"There was a loud bang followed by an even louder roar. I had my eyes open but could see only white as if I were in a cloud. As quickly as the white had appeared, it disappeared and I found myself sitting in the seat, looking at the desert floor about 14,000 feet below. I knew the seat would have to fall down to about 13,000 feet before it would automatically release me and my personal parachute would be automatically opened. I had time so I looked around. To my left I saw a parachute canopy and was elated because I knew my pilot had gotten out, too. But I couldn't figure out why he was under his inflated canopy and I *wasn't!* (There's something very unnerving about seeing other people floating gently down under open parachute canopies when yours is still in the container.) I became very anxious to be under an inflated canopy, too, and was afraid my seat's automatic feature had failed. I reached down to my right side for the manual override handle and pulled it. The seat separated from me and I fell away with my parachute still in the fiberglass container over my head. The 40-pound survival kit was strapped to my rear. I rolled onto my back with a little help from the survival kit, reached for the ripcord on my personnel parachute, and pulled.

"I knew that it wasn't designed to be manually deployed this way and that I might have to pull the apex out of the container. But I was in luck and as soon as I pulled, I saw the multicolored, 28-foot flat circular canopy shoot out of the container. Bang! I was under an inflated canopy about 12,000 feet above the desert floor. I dropped the entire survival kit, pulled the four-line release, and looked around.

"It was at this time that I saw the other two canopies and realized that I had been in a midair collision between our two planes. It was about a 15-minute ride down from 12,000 and I had plenty of time to look around. I saw that one of the airplanes was flying away on fire and that we were still very close to the base where we had taken off. The burning wreckage on the ground gave me a good wind direction indication, so at about 1,500 feet I turned the canopy to face the wind. Just before touching the ground, I pumped the rear risers and did a beautiful, soft, standup landing.

"The other Marines at the base had seen the midair collision and had launched several helicopters to pick us up. They were there by the time I was on the ground. The helicopters took us to the field hospital for a checkup, but no one was hurt except for a few scratches and bruises."

Mark Meyer, the civilian photographer, was probably hurt the most— taking all those beautiful once-in-a-lifetime photographs and then losing his camera during the ejection.

Fate seems to play a big hand in the survival of airmen leaving their disabled aircraft. In March 1964 George Neale, one of the Navy's Blue Angel precision pilots, plunged to his death when he ejected at 200 feet and his parachute failed to open fully. Yet in October 1961 Navy pilot John T. Kryway ejected "on the deck," literally, from the carrier *Roosevelt* and survived with

What's the lowest bailout? Lieutenant B. D. MacFarlane's plane lost power on takeoff from HMS *Albion*, hit the water, and sank. It was then run over by the ship. MacFarlane was somewhere beneath the ship when he *ejected*, but he eventually fought his way to the surface and survived. This sequence of seven photographs shows Lieutenant John T. Kryway ejecting at flight-deck level. His parachute opened in time to check his fall. A helicopter crew retrieved him moments later to discover he had suffered only minor injuries. Kryway was making a normal 130-knot approach to the carrier *Roosevelt* when rough seas caused the deck to dip slightly. The resulting rough landing caused the right wheel to break off and friction ignited the magnesium strut. Although the hook had caught the arresting cable, it broke under the strain and Kryway continued to hurtle down the deck toward a fiery finish. He quickly elected to eject, even at deck level, and survived to fly again. (U.S. Navy)

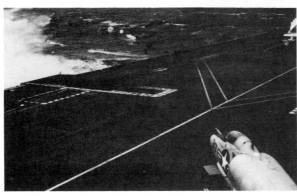

minor injuries. (An unusual sequence of photos was made by Louis J. Cera, USN, a very alert photographer who shot the dramatic event with a K-20 semi-automatic aerial camera.) And Navy Lieutenant Barry Kunkle survived with nothing worse than a broken leg when he ejected at flight-deck level from the carrier *Midway*.

But British Lieutenant B. Macfarlane takes the cake—starting at *below-zero* altitude. Macfarlane of the Royal Navy flew from the British aircraft carrier *HMS Albion* in October 1954. His engine failed as he was catapulted from the deck. The plane struck the water in a nose-down attitude and began to sink. To top this off, the carrier then ran over the plane and shoved it down, broken in half, some twenty feet. At this point Macfarlane triggered his ejection system and blasted free of the wreckage, then released his straps and paddled to the surface with only minor injuries.

And then there's the man who ejected at 1,000 feet but whose chute didn't even come out of the backpack—and who lived to tell about it! In February 1964 Navy pilot Edward A. Dickson fell 1,000 feet, hit in a deep snowdrift, bounced about 50 feet in the air, skidded along the snow, and slammed into a pine tree. Having never bailed out before, he assumed this was routine for an emergency ejection until he discovered his parachute still in the container on his back. His commander, flying another A-4 Skyhawk jet with him, circled over-head and saw Dickson's free fall and bounce. Making the best of the situation, Dickson pulled the ripcord on his chute to get the pack open, then wrapped himself in the parachute to keep warm while waiting for his rescue.

Some men just never give up. On July 11, 1962, Navy Lieutenant Frank K. Ellis ejected from his Cougar jet only 75 feet over the ground near Point Mugu Naval Air Station, California. The story should logically end there, but it doesn't. His chute failed to open, and he crashed through a cluster of eucalyptus trees and into the ground—still in the ejection seat. His left leg was badly mangled, his right leg sheared off below the knee, his back broken, three ribs fractured, and his body covered with multiple burns, cuts, and bruises—but he was still alive. Two months later his remaining leg had to be amputated. He still wouldn't give in. Nine months later he was back at the controls of a T-33B jet taxiing around the field, trying out his two artificial legs and attempting to convince officials he was still capable of flying a plane. Double amputees just don't fly jet planes and the military, while admiring his spirit, said no. He decided to make a parachute jump to prove he could still perform as well as a man with two real legs. On May 19, 1963, he made a jump at Gillespie Field with the San Diego Skydivers. That convinced the right people and, fourteen months after the accident, he was back in the air, flying a variety of aircraft. Frank Ellis became the only double amputee in the history of the Navy to continue on flying status.

Emergency parachute jumping goes back to Polish aeronaut Jordaki Kuparento's leap from his burning balloon over Warsaw in 1808. Even as late as 1919, two men saved their lives by bailing out of the blazing gondola of the *Wingfoot Express* over Chicago.

Emergency parachuting from airplanes starts with Harold Harris—the first man to be awarded the Caterpillar Club pin. Countless thousands have since saved their lives by bailing out.

Stories from Caterpillar Club files and other sources tell of incredible escapes in emergencies when there seemed no chance of survival. Flying Officer Rupert North dived from a Ventura with only a harness on and a QAC (Quick Attachable Chute) parachute in his hand. He snapped it on upside down (the left snap hooked into the right D-ring) by only one snap—then pulled. It worked.

John Vollmer didn't even snap his on at all. He tried unsuccessfully to snap the chute to his harness, but couldn't get either snap into place. Realizing he was about to strike the ground, he pulled with one hand and held on for dear life with the other. The chute was ripped from his hands but at that instant a snap caught in a D-ring and he found himself swinging lazily and safely under the inflated canopy, suspended by one ring.

A gunner and a radioman shared one parachute when they jumped together at 15,000 feet over Germany in 1943. The second man somehow managed to maintain his grip during the opening shock and hung on for more than ten minutes before his strength gave out and he fell the last few hundred feet to his death.

Probably the most incredible story (it's documented and true) is of Joe Herman and John Vivash. One dark night over Germany in 1944, Herman was blown, without his parachute, from his exploding plane at 17,000 feet. Vivash was also blown out but had his parachute on. At about 5,000 feet, Vivash regained consciousness and opened his chute. Herman, fully conscious, bumped into Vivash's body and instinctively hung on. They floated down together on one parachute. They crashed through some brush, Herman on the bottom suffering a couple of broken ribs. They evaded capture for four days before the Germans caught them.

In some cases a jumper, such as Edward A. Dickson, has been unable to get his parachute properly inflated and still has survived. Dr. Richard G. Snyder has made a detailed study of a number of terminal velocity impacts into snow and other substances. It has been estimated that a partially inflated canopy will slow a jumper enough so he can survive in most cases. A canopy which fails to catch air (as when the sleeve fails to clear the canopy) and forms a streamer behind the jumper will still reduce the descent rate appreciably. Joseph Thrift jumped from 12,500 feet and came into a hayfield with a partially inflated

Emergencies develop in sport jumping, too. This unusual sequence of photos was taken by Soviet photographer-parachutist Gennadi Ikonnikov, who was on the field making some routine shots of fellow jumpers loading up and exiting when an emergency developed 3,000 feet overhead. Yuri Belenko had a malfunction, pulled his reserve, which tangled with the main, and began the terrifying descent with a double malfunction. One of the jumpers on the ground looked up and saw the life-or-death struggle. He yelled to fellow jumpers, who grabbed a packing mat and began sprinting toward the impact point. Belenko continued to struggle to clear his malfunction while the men below stretched out the mat and waited. Belenko plummeted into the canvas at bone-crushing speed, ripping the tarp from the hands of his rescuers and knocking them to the ground. When the dust cleared, Belenko was gasping for breath and writhing in pain, but he was alive! Except for an injured leg and minor bruises and abrasions, he was none the worse for wear. These photos are stills taken from Ikonnikov's movie film. (**Soviet Life** magazine)

1

2

3

4

5

6

7

8

9

10

canopy at an estimated 85 mph. He suffered a fractured back, cuts and bruises, and possible internal injuries—but survived. At the hospital, the doctors considered him to be in good condition.

One person who survived without a chute's assistance was Lieutenant Colonel I. M. Chissov of the Soviet Air Force. Chissov had his plane shot out from under him during World War II by several German fighters. He bailed out. Fearing he would be riddled in the air if he opened at 23,000 feet, he decided to delay the opening down to 1,000 feet. During the fall, he lost consciousness and hit with his parachute still intact on a slope covered with some three feet of snow. When he regained consciousness fifteen minutes later, Russian soldiers had reached him and he was taken to a hospital. He had suffered a fractured pelvis and concussion of the spine—and was out of the hospital in three and a half months. He is still active and made his 272nd parachute jump to celebrate his seventieth birthday!

Russian mechanic G. Ochepkov accidentally opened the door of a helicopter and fell out at 1,060 feet. He had previously made 27 parachute jumps but did not have a chute on when he fell through the door. Ochepkov assumed a horizontal face-to-earth position, then opened his heavy quilted jacket and held the flaps in an open position to trap air. Like a flying squirrel he glided himself into a clearing in the woods which was covered with more than six feet of snow. He was knocked unconscious, but recovered consciousness when the helicopter landed, and he climbed, unaided, back into the craft.

During World War II both German and Russian troops were reported to have dropped from low-flying planes into deep snow without the aid of parachutes. Units of the German 4th Army reported to German Intelligence that they had witnessed Soviet troops spilling from low-flying troop carriers without the aid of parachutes during the Yukhnov airborne operation of 1942. One documented case reported that airborne troops were placed in sacks filled with straw!

In 1955, during a large airborne operation in Alaska, an observer saw what appeared to be an unsupported bundle falling from a C-119; no chute deployed from the object. The observer noted that the impact looked like a mortar round exploding in the snow. When aidmen arrived at the spot, they found a young black paratrooper flat on his back at the bottom of a three-foot hole in the snow. He could talk and appeared to be uninjured. However, they took him to a hospital, where it was determined that he had two minor fractures and bruises. He rejoined his unit a few days later.

Again during World War II, Nicholas Alkemade, whose Lancaster bomber and parachute were aflame at 18,000 feet over Germany, decided he would rather die falling than stay and burn to death in the plane. He turned his gun turret around, dropped out into the predawn darkness on March 23, 1944, and plummeted 18,000 feet into a young pine tree. Crashing through the tree, he slammed into 18 inches of snow that had drifted up under it. There was no snow on the ground except under the tree. Not only did he live; he wasn't even seriously injured. Regaining consciousness about three hours after bailing out, he stood up, lit a cigarette, and thanked his lucky stars. After his capture he was treated for burns and had splinters and twigs removed from his flesh. Because he had no parachute, he was accused of being a spy who had hidden his chute. A check of his harness revealed that the liftwebs of the harness he wore (QAC harness) were still tacked down by break cord, indicating the parachute had never been used. Later the wreckage of his plane was found along with the burned parachute still in its metal container beside the gun turret.

What if an airman at 40,000 feet opened his chute immediately on exit, rather than dropping down to lower and more livable air? At such an altitude the temperatures are 70 degrees below zero and oxygen is so scarce that death comes in a matter of seconds. An unintentional jump by Lieutenant Colonel W. R. Lovelace of the Army Air Corps provided some of the answers. Lovelace was not a parachute jumper—he had never made a parachute jump in his life. He was a doctor, a surgeon, to be specific. In 1943 he stepped through the open bomb bay of a B-17 Flying Fortress, where a static line immediately opened his parachute. Lovelace was knocked unconscious by the opening shock, his glove torn from his left hand. He oscillated violently in subzero temperatures, and his hand froze during the long, tortuous descent. The oscillation continued during the entire descent and he suffered from extreme nausea as well as frostbite, shock, and oxygen starvation. While he proved that an airman could survive an opening and descent from that high altitude, his jump also proved the delayed drop to be preferable. The recommended procedure then, as it is today, was to ride the disabled plane down to safer air before bailing out or else delay opening until livable air is reached.

William Stannard, a gunner on a Ventura, was cut off from the exit by flames. Although he managed to get his chute, it was already burning and fell from its container in a melting glob. Flames forced him further back into the rear of the plane. Finally wedged in the extreme tail section, he crouched in a ball with his legs drawn up to his chin and his hands over his face as the flames licked at him. Suddenly the last ten feet of fuselage and tail broke away and fell free of the flaming main section. Stannard found himself trapped inside the tail assembly that glided and fluttered like a leaf. He sat watching the skyline and countryside sweeping by during the 9,000-foot descent. The strange vehicle crashed through some pine trees and, as it ground to a halt, Stannard tumbled out—dazed but not seriously hurt.

A similar incident occurred early in 1972. Yugoslav Airlines hostess Vesna Vulovic found herself at 31,000 feet without an airplane or a parachute. The DC-9 jetliner exploded, killing the other 26 people aboard. Miss Vulovic fell

31,000 feet in the tail section of the plane and spent 40 days recuperating in a Prague hospital. When interviewed four years later, she was working at a desk job in Belgrade and claimed to be "as healthy as my husband or anybody else."

Peter Underdown rode his ejection seat (the parachute never deployed) through an orchard grove in 1954. When his Sabre broke up in flight, his seat broke loose (it was not fired). He smashed through the orchard where his seat—with him still in it—wedged in the fork of an apple tree. He was conscious and yelling, but has no recollection of the three days following the flight. His plane broke up at an estimated 400 mph and he hurtled 2,000 feet to the ground. The trajectory of his seat coincided with the slope of the hill so that the seat struck tree after tree, slowing down until it finally wedged in the fork of the apple tree.

Test pilot George Franklin Smith of Manhattan Beach, California, was the first man to make an emergency jump flying from an airplane at supersonic speed. He ejected from an F-100A Super Sabre jet fighter on February 26, 1955, at an altitude of 6,500 feet and a speed of 777 mph. He experienced a deceleration of 40 G's as the windblast cut his clothes to ribbons and his shoes, socks, helmet, and oxygen mask were stripped away. His parachute was torn in several places but safely lowered the unconscious and half-dead Smith into the ocean off Los Angeles, where he was rescued by a passing boat. He was hospitalized for six months, but survived to fly again. The need for some type of protection during a supersonic bailout was obvious, and Smith's experience spurred the development of a supersonic ejection system.

Among the highest emergency bailouts were those made by John de Salis and Patrick Lowe. As they were flying in a Canberra jet bomber over Derbyshire, England, in April 1958, their plane exploded at 56,000 feet. Both men free-fell down to 10,000 feet, where their parachutes were automatically opened.

In an effort to cope with emergency conditions at supersonic speeds, parachute manufacturers strengthened their parachutes and escape systems. However, with parachutes already able to withstand greater forces than the human body, making the chute even stronger was meaningless. To develop an emergency system that will work instantly when a pilot is ejecting a sluggish plane that falters or fails during takeoff and at very low speeds was difficult, but possible; a number of successful systems had been developed. Jim Hall proved a system that would work at zero altitude and zero airspeed. To develop a system that would work at supersonic speeds was also difficult, but possible. Developing a system that would work rapidly at both low altitude and slow speeds, yet work slowly at high altitudes and high speeds . . . well. Unlike the sport jumper who chooses his speed and altitude, the luckless airman who hits the silk to save his life must go when conditions require it—no matter how fast or how slow, and no matter how high or how low.

Until the supersonic era, the same parachute and same over-the-side technique would work under any situation, but based upon experiences of those few who made emergency exits at near supersonic speeds and lived to tell of it, new methods of escape and new escape systems had to be developed.

Aerospace manufacturers began designing new escape systems that would allow more protection at high speeds. Parachute manufacturers worked closely with them to customize parachutes and automatic devices for opening them. Early Space Shuttle escape systems were designed to operate from speeds of zero to Mach 2.7 and altitudes of from zero to 75,000 feet. After dummy tests indicated success, it was up to a handful of dedicated men to make live tests. These test jumpers set out to prove they had a solution to the emergency jumper's problems—and they staked their lives that they were right.

3. Will It Work?

Test Jumping

Test jumping is more than just strapping on a chute and jumping with it. There was a time when this was the case—when Irvin jumped and proved a free-fall pack would work and when Lieutenant R. A. Caldwell jumped and proved his static arrangement *would not* (it fouled and he was killed).

   If the chute opened and held together, the design was considered a success; if it didn't, they simply buried the victim and tried some other design. But that was many years ago. Chutes were so unreliable then that few were used during World War I.

   Test groups and individuals worked steadily in the succeeding years to develop not only reliable chutes, but other lifesaving equipment and techniques of escape. Planes were going faster and higher; that meant bailouts might be made at great speeds and above the region of breathable air. Parachutes had to be strengthened to withstand high-speed openings or modified in such a way

No matter how good it looks on a drawing board, every new design ultimately must be live-tested. A test jumper must possess an abundance of courage as well as skill and experience if he is to thoroughly evaluate the flight characteristics and offer constructive suggestions for improvement. Here Lee Guilfoyle flies an early Barish Sailwing design. (Jerry Irwin)

that the parachute would open more slowly. By the end of World War II, parachute components no longer needed to be strengthened; the parachute would hold together longer than the man using it.

During World War II the Germans developed the jet airplane. Bailout at jet speeds using a standard quick-opening parachute was, to say the least, uncomfortable . . . and to say the most, fatal. They developed the deployment sleeve that became commonly used in sport parachuting. A sleeve slowed the airman's body and allowed him time to get into a proper position. The sleeve, encasing the canopy, slowed the opening of the canopy so the lines could deploy and the airman could be pulled into the proper position for inflation. The deployment bag operated on the same principle and found its way into paratroop rigs—the T-10—and various emergency parachutes.

As speeds increased, it became impossible for an airman to open a hatch and jump out. Ejection seats came into use. High-altitude exits meant the airman needed to carry an oxygen supply, the bailout bottle, or learn the techniques of falling to lower altitudes and breathable air. Pressure suits were developed to keep the man alive above his physical limits. Higher and higher, faster and faster . . . each development brought new escape problems, and each escape problem brought new equipment, which had to be tested and proved. New techniques of exit and of fall had to be developed. Somebody had to prove to pilots that bailing out was safer than crashing with the plane.

In the early 1920's the odds for survival in an emergency jump were about 50–50; odds for surviving a crash with the plane were about the same. Major E. L. Hoffman and his test group at McCook Field had determined that a free-falling body reaches terminal velocity (when the pull of gravity is equal to the wind resistance) of about 120 mph after falling roughly 1,500 feet. They reasoned, then, that if the pilot bailed out at high speed he would actually slow down as he fell. If he could delay his opening for a brief time, he would be slowing down until he reached 120 mph. In the higher, thinner air he would fall faster, but as he dropped into the denser air of lower altitudes he would continue to slow down until a tolerable opening speed was reached. The theory sounded good, but nobody had made a delayed free fall . . . yet.

Irvin had made a free-fall jump, but how far did he fall before he opened? Just far enough to clear the plane—no more. Pilots and the public in general still had the notion that a delayed fall would result in death or unconsciousness. Besides, slide-rule calculations are one thing—actual performance is something else.

Sergeant Randall Bose decided to prove delayed free falls could be accomplished safely. He delayed his opening for 1,500 feet on one jump and later delayed for 1,800 feet—the first recorded delayed free falls. These jumps were not entirely in the official capacity of test jumper, but more in the form of a bet with some friends who didn't believe it could be done. He made believers of them, collecting on his bet. Bose learned something during his first delayed fall that nobody was aware of—weird things begin to happen at terminal velocity.

His fall was controlled for the first ten seconds, but suddenly everything went crazy. He found himself gyrating, buffeting, swaying from side to side, and generally losing his equilibrium. He even flipped over a couple of times. On his next jump, he was waiting for it, but could do nothing to stop it except pull his ripcord. Although Bose had fallen at terminal velocity only a few seconds, these seconds were enough to prove that "something" happens beyond that twelfth second. Had he fallen another ten seconds he would have encountered the flat spin.

Test jumpers today are aware of the spin and fight it off before it can occur, just as sport jumpers must do. The human body tends to rotate at terminal velocity like a runaway propeller. If the spin is allowed to continue, centrifugal force takes over and the arms and legs are pulled away from the body. In this spread-eagle position, blood is forced away from the center (the body's trunk) into the arms, legs, and head. A red-out (unconsciousness) results.

Spins are erratic, though, and a shifting of the body can cause it to stop and even to counterrotate. Understanding what makes the body spin is the first step in preventing or correcting a spin. One foot or leg higher or lower than the other, one arm or hand higher or lower than the other, or the body twisted slightly—each can cause a spin; there are other factors, but these are basic. In advanced free-fall maneuvers, the jumper learns to use these movements to make turns to the left or right—in competition judging he must do them rapidly and precisely.

The automatic opener is a significant device used to reduce deaths. Most parachutes in use by the military are now equipped with an opener that pulls the ripcord automatically at a given altitude. Depending on the elevation of terrain over which the airman is flying, these openers are normally set barometrically to activate at elevations from 5,000 to 17,000 feet. If the airman bails out below the altitude set on his opener, a timing mechanism pulls the ripcord on the chute. This timer is usually activated automatically as the airman separates from the seat. Timers can be set from as low as five seconds to as much as fifteen seconds. The time delay is necessary to allow the airman to slow down from his initial speed at bailout. If a pilot ejects at high altitude, he simply relies on his automatic opener to take over at the proper time. If he gets in an uncontrollable spin and loses consciousness or cannot pull his ripcord, the automatic opener will do it for him. Although an opening during a flat spin results in twisted suspension lines and often friction burns on the canopy, the lines normally unwind quickly and the canopy inflates properly. Test jumpers learned early in the game that if they encountered a spin that could not be controlled or kept within tolerable limits, the ripcord should be pulled.

After Bose made those first delayed free falls and had a brief brush with the effects of terminal velocity, other test jumpers pushed on for answers to other questions. Some, like Art Starnes and Russia's Boris Kharakhonoff, experimented with delayed fall. Starnes made a free fall from 30,800 feet loaded with nearly 100 pounds of equipment that included, in addition to his two parachutes, a stopwatch, an altimeter, a shortwave radio, a 16 mm movie camera, various medical sensors, and other odds and ends. The six-mile free-fall record that he set in 1940 was broken the next year by Kharakhonoff's drop from 40,813 feet. Both men proved that free falls from high altitudes could be made safely.

For more than thirty years the major parachute-testing operations were conducted at McCook Field, Dayton, Ohio, where Irvin had made the world's first free-fall jump to prove the Model A parachute would work. The result of his test was that parachutes were made acceptable to the military and optional for all pilots. When young Lieutenant Harold Harris bailed out and saved his life with that same type of parachute in 1922, he proved not only that the parachute would work, but that it was practical for pilots in an emergency. As a result of Lieutenant Harris's experience, parachutes were made mandatory a year later.

In 1952 the parachute test center was moved to El Centro, California. This was done to consolidate the efforts of the Air Force with those at the Navy Auxiliary Air Station in El Centro. The unit became the Joint Department of Defense Parachute Testing Center.

Four men's names are synonymous with parachute testing there. They worked together for fifteen years and have become known as "the jumping warrants" as each climbed the promotion ladder to become chief warrant officers.

Victor A. James, who made his first jump at an airshow, went on to test the overall USAF ejection seat system with a high-speed bailout from a P-80 jet. He also set a high-altitude record free fall (for the 1950's) by bailing out at 38,000 feet and free-falling 24,000 feet before opening his chute. The tests were made to determine if a man should free-fall with or without his seat to his opening altitude.

Mitchell Kanowski began jumping at Airborne Infantry School at Fort Benning, Georgia, where one of his duties was to test captured enemy parachutes. At El Centro he went on to test the German ribbon design, which was ultimately adopted and used in the experimental high-altitude research rocket planes.

Isadore Rosenberg was the only one to begin his testing career as just that—a test jumper. He volunteered at Wright-Patterson Air Force Base after seeing a notice on the bulletin board asking for volunteers to take part in some parachute testing programs. His contributions, in addition to test jumping himself, include numerous designs and modifications for survival in low-altitude escapes from both jet and conventional propeller-driven craft.

Lawrence Lambert started parachuting as a flying circus barnstormer before entering the service. He received the Cheney Award for his outstanding work testing the first USAF ejection seat system. He later worked with Colonel John P. Stapp in the deceleration tests at old Muroc Air Base and, still later, assisted in training Captain Joe Kittinger, who went on to set the world's unofficial record for high-altitude jump.

On November 16, 1959, Captain Joseph William Kittinger, Jr., 32, set a high-altitude record parachute jump when he free-fell from a balloon-supported open gondola 76,400 feet over the Air Force Missile Development Center, Holloman Air Force Base, New Mexico. It was not his first—he had made one emergency bailout and nearly fifty intentional jumps—but it was very nearly his last. This was the first of three extremely high jumps in Project Excelsior, intended to

Captain Joseph W. Kittinger gets a final check of equipment in the predawn hours before his record-breaking balloon ascent and parachute jump. (U.S. Air Force)

test high-altitude bailout survival clothing and equipment in a special biospace research task developed by the Air Research and Development Command.

On the Excelsior I jump, Kittinger stepped out at 76,000 feet—5,000 feet higher than a man had even been in an open gondola. At 60,000 feet his body reached a terminal velocity of 423 mph. The outside air was 104 degrees below zero. Something happened to his stabilization chute and it tangled around his body, where it fluttered uselessly. Kittinger controlled his body as much as he could in the thin air, but this was not enough and, despite all his efforts, he found himself building up into a deadly flat spin. He found himself paralyzed by the centrifugal force whirling him around and eventually he lost consciousness. When he regained consciousness, he was floating safely to earth under his automatically deployed reserve chute. His automatically opened main had fouled in the stabilization chute, then his reserve automatically deployed and tangled with the main. The reserve chute's pilot chute caught, preventing the canopy from inflating. However, Francis Beaupre, designer of the stabilization chute and Leo

Stevens Medal winner, had anticipated such an emergency and substituted a weaker bridle cord from the apex to the pilot chute. This bridle cord broke when forces of falling built up, and the reserve canopy pulled free and inflated properly.

Later examination showed that Kittinger had accidentally started his timer on his stabilization chute without realizing it when he stood up to jump. He delayed exit some ten or eleven seconds while starting cameras and pulling other releases. When he stepped from the gondola, instead of having sixteen seconds of fall before the pilot chute would pop and deploy his 6-foot stabilization chute, he had only two or three. This was not sufficient time to build up the speed needed to properly extend and inflate the chute. It simply bobbled around his body and entangled itself completely before speed built up to a functional level, and by then it was too late.

Kittinger went up to make the Excelsior II flight and jump just 25 days after the first. This time everything went exactly as planned. Exactly fourteen seconds after stepping out, he had reached a speed of 300 mph. His timer went off, and the stabilization chute deployed perfectly. He fell in a perfectly stable position down to 18,000 feet, where his main canopy deployed and lowered him to the ground 12 minutes and 32 seconds after exit. With Excelsior II going perfectly, he moved on to Excelsior III—the big one.

On August 16, 1960, Kittinger reached an altitude of 102,800 feet. Excelsior III had taken him higher than any man had ever been in a balloon. In 1957 he had taken part in Project Manhigh, making the first ascent in a sealed gondola and reaching 96,000 feet. He was followed later by Lieutenant Colonel David G. Simons, who reached 102,000 feet. Lieutenant Clifton McClure, in the same project, later reached 99,000 feet. But these three flights were in enclosed gondolas. This time the pilot was completely exposed to the elements except for his pressurized space suit and survival equipment.

The equipment Kittinger wore on this jump exactly duplicated his weight —150 pounds. His 300-pound bulk required the efforts of several assistants when he entered the open gondola. However, at 102,800 feet he weighed three pounds less. Gravity decreases one percent for each 100,000 of altitude.

Like an overstuffed teddy bear, Kittinger struggled to his feet, shuffled to the doorway and hopped out nearly twenty miles above New Mexico.

Sixteen seconds after he left the gondola of Excelsior III, a timer fired to release the Beaupre stabilization parachute. The 6-foot diameter parachute had no perceivable effect on his fall—no shock—and he wondered if it was working or if he should pull his manual override. Then he felt the gentle tugging that assured him the chute was out and working properly—he was no longer doing a slow roll but had stabilized in a face-to-earth position. Thirty seconds after his exit he passed through the 90,000-foot mark and reached his top speed of

Although Captain Kittinger deployed a 6-foot stabilization parachute after sixteen seconds of free fall, he continued to accelerate for the first thirty seconds and reached a top speed of 614 mph. It took him a total of 13 minutes and 45 seconds to cover the 102,800 feet. (U.S. Air Force)

614 mph! He spoke into his tape recorder as he fell, giving readings from the stopwatch and altimeter and making remarks on the overall situation, his feelings, and the functioning of the automatic equipment. His chute, a standard 28-foot backpack, automatically deployed at 18,000 feet after he had fallen for four and one half minutes. As he reached the 1,000-foot level, he released some of his 150 pounds of equipment, and a static-line deployed parachute lowered it separately to the desert floor. Kittinger landed in the soft warm sand 13 minutes and 45 seconds after exit. His jump had gone so perfectly that the follow-up jump by Sergeant Post was cancelled as unnecessary. He had proven that a human being and equipment can function and survive in the hostile realm of outer space.

An ironic note is the fact that, although both his balloon ascent and his jump were record-breakers, they could not be officially recognized as such.

Three times Nick Piantanida attempted to reach the outer limits of our atmosphere where he planned to break the sonic barrier in free fall with no stabilization chute. He once reached 123,000 feet, but equipment failure foiled him and his third attempt was fatal. (SPACE, Inc.)

To set an official balloon record, the occupant must both ascend and descend in the balloon; Joe had not. To set an official parachute record, designated representatives of FAI must witness the jump and special recording barographs must be carried on the drop, and neither of these requirements had been met. But Kittinger's goal was not to set official records or gain personal glory; it was to test equipment. He accomplished that.

Ordinarily, a jump such as Kittinger's could be made only by military people, working for Uncle Sam and supported by millions of federal dollars, but Nicholas J. Piantanida, 33, was no ordinary man. He became interested in the problems of high-altitude bailouts and decided to do some testing of his own. He wanted to prove that a jumper, employing ordinary skydiving techniques of controlled free fall, could safely make the jump without any stabilization chute. He intended to break the speed of sound with nothing but his 6-foot, 2-inch, 200-pound body. This sounded pretty hazardous to most people, but Nick began recruiting support for his project.

While it was true that Nick was not a trained astronaut or military test jumper, he was not entirely inexperienced or unfamiliar with the subject of flight and parachuting. He was a licensed pilot, rated for single-engine, multi-engine, and balloons. He had more than 400 parachute jumps to his credit and held a Class D (expert) parachutist's license. His greatest qualification, however, was his determination. It began to pay off when he teamed up with parachuting's super salesman, Jacques Istel.

By August 1965, SPACE, Inc., was formed. It stood for Survival Programs Above Common Environment and consisted of three principals: Parachutes Incorporated, Pioneer Parachute Company, and Piantanida.

SPACE began working on the strato-jump project. For civilians to work up a program of this magnitude was unthinkable. The money required for training, parachutes, spacesuits, instruments, balloon, helium, and dozens of other items would be well beyond the reach of any private enterprise. SPACE representatives—Piantanida and Istel taking a major role—began listing their objectives, then sought out those companies who could best profit from the project. Strato-jump objectives were: (1) To establish that a trained parachutist can free-fall from altitudes in excess of 100,000 feet without the use of stabilizing devices. (2) To investigate the effects of transonic speeds on the human body in free fall. (3) To gain for the United States the world's free-fall altitude parachuting record. (4) To surpass the manned-balloon altitude record.

SPACE went on to explain the value of these objectives. If they could prove that a properly trained man can free-fall safely from great altitudes without any stabilization device, the current system of emergency procedures could be greatly simplified. Normally, in the event of an emergency, the airman rides his disabled aircraft (or part of it) down to altitudes of less than 30,000 feet before getting out. In the event of fire or structural failure this is not always possible. Special free-fall training could mean the difference of life and death and, aside from saving a man's life, our government cannot afford to lose its financial investment. They pointed to the fact that the United States had invested $6.5 million dollars in each astronaut.

What happens to a man when he breaks through the sound barrier with his body? The Pioneer Parachute Company engineers computed that on a jump from 120,000 feet, the parachutist should reach a maximum speed of approximately Mach 1.1 (750 mph) in the vicinity of 90,000 feet. They pointed out that at speeds near and above Mach 1, the air flow may differ from what is normally experienced in free fall. A safety device would be available, however. In the event control could not be maintained, a small drogue chute would be deployed to slow the free-fall speed and reduce the dynamic pressure against the jumper's body. General Electric's Re-Entry Systems Department in Philadelphia sent equipment and a team of engineers and technicians to measure the free-fall

With the increased activities in hang gliding, a significant number of pilots were being injured or killed—frequently because of structural failure in flight. A parachute system was needed that would function quickly, even at very low altitudes, and still deploy around the tangled pieces of tubing and fabric. Therefore, Jim Handbury of Advanced Air Sports designed, built, and test-jumped the system to prove its reliability. (Carl Boenish)

velocity precisely. This would be accomplished by a small transmitter mounted on the rear of the reserve parachute container and a receiver positioned on the ground.

In addition to the actual scientific and technical value of the jump, there was the nationalism felt by many concerned. The Russians still held the official high-altitude parachute record. Eugene Andreev set the record on November 1, 1962, near Volsk, Russia, when he jumped from 83,523.41 feet. Kittinger's jump was higher, but, because it was not properly monitored by the Federation Aeronautique Internationale, it was not accepted as an official record, nor could SPACE, Inc., break the world's balloon record set in May 1961 by Commander Malcolm D. Ross, USNR, when he reached an altitude of 113,739.9 feet. Although Nick would go higher, he must return with the balloon in order to establish an official balloon record. Nick would return by parachute instead. The idea picked up momentum and Piantanida's enthusiasm spread to others.

Nick took extensive training in preparation for his adventure. The Air Force cooperated to the extent that they furnished pressure-suit training and initial physiological training at Tyndall Air Force Base at Panama City, Florida. Considerable additional physiological training and a cold chamber run, at minus 73 degrees Fahrenheit, were received at the Civil Aeromedical Research Institute, Federal Aviation Administration, in Oklahoma City. His parachute training was conducted at Parachutes Incorporated's Lakewood Sport Parachuting Center at Lakewood, New Jersey. There, with the guidance of Lee Guilfoyle, the center's manager, and other staff people, Nick made high-altitude drops with and without his pressure suit and purposely practiced recovering from spins.

Meanwhile, Istel and other members of SPACE, Inc., were lining up the necessary equipment. Some items were donated outright, some were provided at cost or less. Piantanida's instrumentation included an electric control panel, an absolute pressure gauge for determining altitude, two temperature gauges to read both inside and outside air temperature, and a clock. The parachutes, harness, and containers were especially designed, manufactured and furnished for the project by Pioneer Parachute Company of Manchester, Connecticut, a partner in SPACE, Inc. His main canopy was, of course, Pioneer's highly maneuverable, slow-descending Para-Commander. The reserve was a 28-foot military type, modified for steering, if that became necessary. He also had a 6-foot hemisflo drogue chute mounted in a tandem pack along with the main chute on his back, just in case it became necessary to use it. He wore the reserve on the front with an altimeter and stopwatch mounted on it.

The full pressure suit was basically an Air Force type, especially constructed and modified for this project by the David Clark Co. of Worcester, Massachusetts. David Clark also built NASA's Gemini suits. Nick wore electrically heated mittens and socks as well as a helmet with an electrically heated visor.

The Firewel Company of Buffalo, New York, furnished the oxygen systems. Four separate oxygen systems were designed and assembled for the project. Both main and reserve breathing systems were installed on board the gondola along with an oxygen ventilation system for cooling the suit in the event of a heat buildup. A bailout unit of oxygen was carried inside the main parachute container and was to be activated a few minutes prior to the actual jump.

Automatic openers were installed in both the main and reserve parachutes. Both were model FF-1, manufactured and provided for the project by U.S. Gauge, Sellersville, Pennsylvania. The main was set to activate at 6,500 feet, with the reserve set for 4,000 feet. If necessary, the openers could be overridden for a manual pull higher if the jumper found himself over a congested area and needed more time and maneuvering room in the sky.

Communications systems involved three radios—one main and two backup units. A command receiver was used to control the balloon functions and, via this receiver, ballast could be dropped or the flight terminated. Both Nick and the ground control people could operate these functions. During free fall Nick was to transmit his reactions into a tape recorder carried in a pocket on the leg of his pressure suit.

Nick would make three attempts at his goal. All three would be unsuccessful—the last one, fatal.

Strato-Jump I was a flight launched from New Brighton, Minnesota, on October 22, 1965. The attempt ended when the 3,700,000-cubic-foot balloon burst over St. Paul, Minnesota. He had just passed the 22,700-foot level when a six-knot wind sheer caught his balloon and shredded it. A ground signal released the gondola from the burst balloon and it descended under the large parachute with Nick in it. At 10,000 feet, Nick decided to bail out and try to steer his personnel chute out of the congested area of St. Paul. In true Dumbo Willans tradition, he landed, boiling mad but safe, in the city dump. On this particular flight, balloon construction and flight operations were conducted by the Applied Science Division of Litton Industries, St. Paul, Minnesota. Nick had jumped from higher than that—up to 36,000 feet—during his training jumps at Lakewood Parachuting Center.

The next try was Strato-Jump II, made February 2, 1966, from Sioux Falls, South Dakota. Raven Industries of Sioux Falls built the balloon and handled the launch, tracking, and recovery operations. The balloon was constructed of 3/4 mil polyethylene film, 340 feet long and 228 feet in diameter. At peak altitude the helium-filled balloon contained a volume of 5 million cubic feet. Projected plans were for the balloon to reach between 120,000 and 122,000 feet. Nick actually got to 123,500 feet—the highest a man had ever been in a balloon. The gondola was a nonpressurized, expanded polystyrene enclosed cube, measuring 4 by 4 by 5-1/2 feet. The frame was of welded tubular aluminum.

The balloon was not attached to the gondola, but rather to the apex of a 46-foot parachute. The parachute was then attached to the gondola. Engineers, ready for any emergency, figured the gondola could descend, with Piantanida in it, at a rate of 25 feet per second, which is roughly equivalent to a landing in some of those older, "hot" modifications—hard, but tolerable. Nick weighed a solid 200 pounds to begin with, and his equipment added another 160 pounds to give him a total of 360 pounds inside the gondola. Everything went off perfectly as Nick ascended to a record-breaking altitude.

The launch took place at 12:11 P.M. and at 1:53 Nick reported his altimeter reading as 120,500 feet. Then he began his five-minute countdown to jump. At jump-minus-three, he reported putting his visor down and activating his G.E. oscillator (the transmitter used to record his rate of fall). At jump-minus-two, he released his seat belt, reset the gondola's automatic timer for another fifteen minutes (when it would automatically release itself from the balloon), and activated his oxygen bailout unit. At jump-minus-one, he tried to disconnect his main oxygen supply—his last link with the gondola before the jump. But the connection was frozen, and with his heavy mittens, he could not manage to disconnect. He struggled for ten minutes trying to get the hose loose so he could make his long-dreamed-of jump. For lack of a suitable wrench, he simply could not get the fitting released.

He became almost frantic. He huffed and puffed, he cursed and prayed, but no matter how he tried, the main hose could not be disconnected.

Finally it became evident that he could not disconnect. If he struggled too hard and tore the hose loose, he would instantly lose the pressure from his suit. A loss of pressure at even *half* this altitude would be fatal. The blood would boil in his veins and he would explode. He had no choice now but to give up and ride back, still attached to his main oxygen supply and to the gondola.

Ed Yost of Raven Industries, the ground control director, notified Nick that they would give him a countdown and then release his gondola from the balloon. First, however, he must get seated and reconnect his seat belt. Nick couldn't fasten his seat belt because the heavy mittens made even a simple thing like that impossible. This became his greatest concern now, because without being fastened in the gondola, he could easily tumble out during the drop. Nick knew that the gondola would fall for several thousand feet before the parachute would inflate, and the gondola would probably be spinning and tumbling during the fall. The opening shock of the gondola's parachute would be extremely great. From the results of Kittinger's epic jump and other tests during that time, it was felt that a parachute opening at high speed and extremely high altitude would be beyond the survival capabilities of a human being. Nick was about to find out. He braced himself as best he could and hung on for dear life.

Yost gave the countdown and released the gondola at 2:12 P.M. from an altitude of 123,500 feet. For the next 35 seconds the gondola hurtled faster and faster and Nick hung on, dreading the opening shock. If the gondola happened to be on its side with the open part down when the chute opened, Nick would be hurtled out. If he hurtled out, his oxygen hose would be ripped loose, his space-suit would depressurize, and he would die in seconds. His strength was dwindling rapidly. But for some reason, the gondola did not tumble or spin. It dropped stable as a rock for 25,500 feet. It reached a top speed of 600 mph or 80 percent of terminal velocity. At 98,000 feet the canopy caught air and inflated. Nick later said the opening was no more uncomfortable than a normal terminal velocity opening in free fall.

For the next 31 minutes he rode the gondola down as it oscillated violently from side to side through strong upper winds. Periods of nausea overtook him as the gondola swung back and forth like a giant pendulum. Although he deactivated his reserve, he could not disarm his main canopy, which was set to open at 6,500 feet. He wanted to bail out at a lower altitude but could not because he still could not get the oxygen hose loose. Realizing the landing would be hard, Jacques Istel radioed Nick to put his main chute under him and stand on it to help absorb the landing shock. At 2:45 he smashed into the ground. A hard, but safe landing.

Nick stayed in the gondola and finally pried the hose loose with a knife before the recovery crew reached him. Although the flight was a failure in terms of his jump, Nick proved two important facts: that an object will not tumble or spin from high altitudes unless induced by some other force than just falling, and that the opening shock at high speed and high altitude is well within the limits of human endurance. The need for pressure suits that allow more maneuverability was obvious. More flexible gloves and suits would have to be developed. Three months later Strato-Jump III began, early on the morning of May 6, 1966. Nick's wife, Janice, was there to wave to him and breathe a prayer for him as he lifted off and began the ascent.

Sixty minutes after launch, he had reached 57,000 feet. Over the intercom was heard a gush of air and a frantic, indistinguishable word, followed by a choked cry of "Emergency!" Instantly, the ground crew released the balloon and the gondola began the 26-minute descent with the unconscious Nick inside.

Apparently his face shield had blown out of the pressure suit. Later evidence indicated Nick had acted quickly to release his belt and tear loose connections in an attempt to dive over the side and reach life-sustaining air. If he had been only a few thousand feet higher his blood would have boiled and he would have died within seconds. As it was, he was without oxygen, where unconsciousness occurs within a few seconds.

During the descent, Nick's flight surgeon flew nearby and landed moments before the gondola touched down. He was at Nick's side within 30 seconds. Nick was in a coma from oxygen starvation. At the hospital he was given oxygen in an attempt to restore his systems, but the damage was irreparable. He was moved to other hospitals for more intensive care, but on August 29, 1966, almost four months after the attempt, Nick Piantanida died without ever regaining consciousness. His courage and personal sacrifice will never be forgotten.

There are dozens of other test jumpers who are highly respected and experienced. Self-sacrifice has been characteristic of test jumpers since the beginning. The development of safe equipment to save the lives of others remains their first concern, and their own skins take second place. When the exhibition jumper attempts some harebrained stunt, he gets money and glory. When a test jumper does something even more spectacular, he gets little more than experience and a sense of satisfaction.

Before the test jumper puts a new design to the test and makes a live jump, machines such as this whirl tower are used to check strength, stability, and other vital characteristics. Wind tunnel tests are made too. (Pioneer Parachute Co.)

Before live-test jumps are made on a new design, it is tested on machines and on dummy drops. Although instrumented dummies are used in the initial phases of development of any parachute or escape system, ultimately a human being must prove equipment. There are two main reasons for this. First, an instrumented dummy does not fall or respond like a human being and no amount of instrumentation can detect every minute detail of performance. Second, no pilot or airman wearing this equipment likes to think it works only in theory on the drawing board or on a dummy. He wants to know it has been proved by many successful jumps by real, live people.

The Vortex Ring parachute was designed by David Barish, who also designed the Barish Sailwing. The Vortex Ring chute looks more like a ragged malfunction than a parachute and has all the characteristics of a rotating Mae West. It was designed for nonpersonal use, and twelve live tests were made to see what potential existed for sport use. Jacques Istel made two jumps with it at the Orange Sport Parachute Center and had to cut away from one malfunction. Nate Pond made ten jumps into Long Island Sound off New London, Connecticut. Pond chose to jump over water after seeing how hard Istel landed on earlier jumps. There were two risers from the harness going up to a ball-bearing swivel about three feet above his head. The parachute rotates as it descends, and the jumper tends to counterrotate unless he can extend his arms and deflect air with

Nate Pond is seen here making one of several test jumps on the Vortex Ring parachute designed by David Barish. Pond made this jump into Long Island Sound off New London, Connecticut. (Pioneer Parachute Co.)

the hands to control the spinning, as Pond discovered. Pond had to cut away from one malfunction out of ten jumps and reported that if one of the wings malfunctioned, it would tangle with the others due to the rotation.

Vince Mazza made the first jet ejection from a P-80 and later made a record-breaking parachute drop from 42,176 feet. On that jump he weighed 347 pounds, including his equipment. Ed Sperry and Hank Neilsen broke Mazza's record when they made some downward ejections in 1954 from an altitude of 45,200 feet. Others working on the downward ejection seat then were Chic Henderson and George Post.

Sergeant George Post received the Distinguished Flying Cross for his part in these first downward ejections. He was the first enlisted man to leave a B-47 jet bomber by that method. He and fellow test jumpers, Captain Harry Collins and Ray Madson, made numerous high-altitude bailouts and went on to test equipment used on extremely high altitudes.

While working with Raven Industries in the manufacture of the strato-

Nick Piantanida made the first manned jump of a plastic film parachute and reported it to be very stable. By pulling down on a riser of this 37.5-foot model, he demonstrated a controlled 360-degree turn in ten seconds. (Raven Industries, Inc.)

jump balloon, Nick Piantanida also test-jumped some unique plastic parachutes developed by Raven. These parachutes, designated "Raven-Plus," were inexpensive, very stable, and extremely lightweight, and ranged in size from 8 inches to 80 feet in diameter. Raven has also made parachutes of similar design in special plastic films that are water soluble. These are intended for applications to limited warfare and one-time use. After a cargo drop, the canopies slowly degrade as atmospheric moisture is absorbed.

Another experiment at Raven Industries, developed by senior engineer Russell A. Pohl, offered the pilot a choice of parachute or balloon. It was designed to help rescue pilots shot down over North Vietnam or other enemy territory. The pilot would eject and, after his seat fell away, pull a ripcord to inflate a hot-air balloon. Plans called for the balloon to be inflated with air by the fall of the airman, then a bottle of compressed propane gas would begin burning automatically. The hot air would fill the bag, slow the descent to a stop, and then lift the airman to the 5,000-foot level, where he would wait for a recovery plane to pick him up. The recovery system, conducted by C-130 cargo planes, was successfully accomplished by using two 35-foot steel poles and a hook and loop assembly. The rescue pilot would fly the recovery plane over the downed airman, and the balloon collapsed as the hook and loop assembly engaged it. An energy-absorbing winch in the recovery plane took the shock and then reeled the pilot and collapsed balloon aboard.

In another experiment, Charles M. Alexander volunteered to test a technique of midair recovery of a parachute. In September 1966 Alexander, a project engineer for Pioneer, became the first person to be recovered from midair. He jumped at 9,000 feet and was recovered at 8,000 feet by pilot Arnold Olsen, flying a C-122 for All American Engineering Company, manufacturer of the airborne retrieval equipment. Extending up from Alexander's modified C-9 main canopy was a nylon load line 70 feet long with a breaking strength of 4,000 pounds. At the upper end of the line was an 11-foot-diameter guide surface target or engagement chute that was snagged by the recovery plane. The special energy-absorbing line and winch were the secret of the system's success.

There are obviously too many test jumpers—military and civilian—to begin to discuss them all. Certain ones stand out for special achievements that should be recognized here. I have had the good fortune and pleasure of personally meeting and jumping with some of the nation's top test jumpers; there is no finer group of men alive today.

Pioneer Parachute Company engineer Charles Alexander, with more than 860 jumps, is reeled into the plane after the world's first human midair recovery. (All American Engineering)

Sergeant James A. Howell is shown shortly after his test drop of the B-seat ejection system in September 1960. A few months later he became the first person to live-test the ejection system at a speed of 558 mph. Howell was twice awarded the Distinguished Flying Cross for his outstanding work. (U.S. Air Force)

On June 6, 1961, Sergeant James A. Howell became the first man to live-test the supersonic ejection seat. He ejected from an F-106B interceptor traveling at 558 mph at 22,000 feet over Holloman AFMDC, New Mexico. The ejection seat used in this test was the F-106 advanced escape system commonly known as the "B" seat, or supersonic seat. The test was an unqualified success that climaxed a four-and-a-half-year program to develop a safe pilot escape system for high-speed aircraft. Less than five months later he made the first live-test ejection of the toboggan-like rescue vehicle. One of the best liked and most respected men in the business of test jumping, Howell has twice been awarded the Distinguished Flying Cross.

Early in 1956 the need for a high-speed escape system was reaching a critical stage as faster and faster planes were being developed. The Air Force requested the aircraft industry to join with equipment manufacturers to develop such a system. The group, known as the Industry Crew Escape Systems Committee, consisted of representatives from fourteen aircraft and equipment companies. The seat that resulted from their labors had the unique feature of rotating backward as it emerged from the aircraft so that when launched, the pilot was in a supine position. It was propelled away from the aircraft by a rocket and stabilized against tumbling by two long 3-inch-diameter booms extending aft along the flight path. The action of these booms was similar to that of the stick on a skyrocket.

After the ejection, Howell plummeted 7,000 feet in a 40-second free fall until an explosive charge—triggered by barometric pressure—cut the shoulder straps and lap belts holding him to the seat. It also fired a weight that pulled out a small parachute. The small chute hoisted Howell from the seat and opened a conventional parachute on his back. Eight minutes after beginning his 4-1/2-mile drop—his four hundredth for the Air Force—he was on the ground.

Sergeant Thomas H. Rolf was one of the men who shared the earlier testing with Howell. He rode the seat down a tilting steel and wood rack and out the back of a C-130 Lockheed Hercules cargo plane. These were test drops prior to installation systems for actual ejections. Some of the work done by test jumpers is classified and cannot be released to the general public.

Testing a variety of the multistage personnel parachutes that are used by our astronauts was a job that fell to other test jumpers such as Sergeant William E. Powers, Jr., and Sergeant Richard Marcum, the two top jumpers in the country, according to fellow jumper Howell.

Test drops were unusually complex, involving extremes in altitude, with multistage, four-timer systems, all self-contained and both fully automatic and manually operated. On one particular drop, shortly after his exit, Sergeant Powers experienced a malfunction in his first-stage chute, then his main also failed. The plastic mouth cover taped over his nose began sticking to his face, making breathing almost impossible. He was tumbling out of control. Because of his full-pressure spacesuit and survival kits, his movements were hampered. He could not free his breathing because of the space helmet and faceplate, and his malfunctioned equipment wrapped him into a neat package. He somehow managed to keep a cool head and quickly corrected his difficulties.

Sergeant Powers did not limit his parachuting only to testing—which he began back in 1958. He was active in the sport of parachuting, a member of the Parachute Club of America (now U.S.P.A.), an area safety officer, holder of a D-license (expert), and organizer-instructor of local clubs.

There is little comparison between sport jumping equipment and techniques and those involved in testing. The sport jumper usually drops from a slow-moving plane, often at less than 10,000 feet, and opens at 2,500 to 2,000 feet with a device that slows deployment, requiring three to four seconds to completely inflate. The test jumper may drop from extremely high altitudes and at high speeds and have his chute opened instantly by a ballistic slug at no less than 14,500 feet. It is generally agreed that opening shock is greater at higher altitudes than in lower, denser air. Howell and others of his group made these drops

Sergeant William E. Powers, Jr., in the Gemini pressure suit and gear just prior to a drop. On this drop his parachutes malfunctioned and his plastic mouth cover made breathing nearly impossible. He somehow overcame the problems and landed safely. (U.S. Air Force)

in standard 28-foot flat circular canopies without any deployment device. Where there is little discomfort during the opening of a sport parachute, the test jumper sometimes wears a protective metal-frame chest protector to keep his ribs from being crushed during the opening of some chutes, particularly when wearing the reserve parachute. The windblast alone is sometimes great enough during high-speed ejections to require extra protection for the jumper. Reserves must be shielded by a windblast cover that is automatically released after the jumper's speed has decelerated. Some test jumpers have tested equipment without the benefit of the reserve because it would not have time to deploy if the main malfunctioned.

Such a man is James C. Hall, for many years an executive of ParaVentures and later Parachuting Associates, Inc., of Los Angeles. Hall made the first human test of the free world's only operational zero altitude/zero airspeed ejection seat, developed by the Weber Aircraft Company. In one year, 1964, there were 35 airmen killed during takeoff or landing when their aircraft developed trouble on the runway. In many cases the pilots ejected but their escape systems could not operate in time.

Hall set out to prove that this zero-zero system would work in time. He initiated the entire sequence by pulling the ejection handle of his seat in a simulated cockpit as it sat stationary, anchored to the ground. An explosive charge shot him straight up from the cockpit. As he cleared the cockpit, a 4,500-pound thrust rocket burned for less than a second to shove him 400 feet into the air in forward flight at an angle of about 60 degrees. Within two seconds after leaving the ground-based platform, the seat and man automatically separated. The parachute deployment gun fired a 13-ounce slug that extracted a small drogue chute, and the main 28-foot-diameter chute inflated. He was hanging about 350 feet in the air; some 400 feet horizontally from his blast-off point. Twenty-five seconds after ejection, he landed safely in a small pond. He had purposely chosen to be shot into the pond in the event anything failed, since he wore no reserve parachute and would not have had time to use it if he had.

A major in the Air Force Reserve, Hall received the highest award in the field of parachuting safety, the Leo Stevens Parachute Medal, for the development of an advanced free-fall parachuting instruction method and for perfecting the method.

Hall was co-inventor of the Air Force's emergency parachuting safety aid, the "four line cut" parachute canopy modification. When the jumper cuts the two inside suspension lines on each rear riser (numbers 2 and 1; 28 and 27), a standard 28-foot canopy develops steerable characteristics so the airman can avoid dangerous obstacles and steer his canopy by pulling down on left or right risers.

One of the interesting developments in parachuting was the Parawing, invented by Dr. Francis Rogallo, aerodynamicist for NASA. Loy Brydon, D-12

Jim Hall tests the F-106 ejection seat in a zero-zero situation. He wore no reserve parachute since there would be no time to use it if the system failed. Hall received the Leo Stevens award for his contributions to safe parachuting. (Parachuting Associates, Inc.)

(the twelfth recipient of the Class D expert license), the first American to make 1,000 free falls and developer of free-fall techniques and parachute modifications, made the first live test jump of the Rogallo Parawing, an all-flexible deployable glider-like parachute. The test was made in March 1966 at Fort Bragg, North Carolina. Others participating in the evaluation jumps were Lieutenant Jack Helms, Captain James Perry, Master Sergeant Harry Lewis, and Staff Sergeant Richard Peyton.

Pioneer Parachute Company built two wings for testing, while Irvin Para-Space Center built two others of slightly different design. Sergeant Lewis made the first live test of the Irvin design.

Early in 1964, tests were made to evaluate the Ballute as a safety device for the Gemini astronauts. Goodyear Aerospace developed the Ballute device under contract to McDonnell Aircraft Corporation, prime contractor for NASA's Project Gemini. The aluminum-coated, nylon device inflates to 48 inches in diameter and acts as a stabilizer until the astronaut reaches an altitude where the conventional parachute is deployed. During training for the Gemini mission, astronauts were required to make several parachute descents into water to test survival techniques. Although NASA did not require any actual parachute

The Ballute is test-jumped by Colonel Clyde S. Cherry, commanding officer of the 6511th Test Group (Parachute) at the Naval Air Facility, El Centro, California. Recording the action with his helmet-mounted camera is Chief Warrant Officer Charles O. Laine. (Goodyear)

Late astronaut Virgil Grissom is pictured with the Pioneer Parasail. Towed behind a boat, the Parasail lifts like a kite, but descends like a standard parachute. (NASA)

Loy Brydon, the first American to log 1,000 free-falls, makes the first live-test jump of the Rogallo Parawing, an all-flexible deployable glider. From this basic design a number of modifications have been developed. (Irvin Para-Space Center)

jumps, they did require extensive training in parachute descents. The Parasail was used; billed as "the parachute that goes up," when towed behind a boat it lifts like a kite, but descends like a standard parachute. Astronauts on Apollo missions wore no parachutes.

Cool action under the most extreme stress situations exemplifies the skill and courage of the test jumper. He meets every challenge, every danger, with a sense of determination to prove or disprove the worth of a particular design. Daredevils of the circuses—with their human cannonball acts or highwire stunts —are putting on a show before thousands of people. The test jumper puts on his "act" before a handful of people in the air and on the ground.

4. As the Pro Goes

Professional Parachuting

Professional parachuting covers a lot of territory. To do more than scratch the surface is impossible in a brief space.

Among the early pros, when the sport was really catching on in the United States, were Jim Hall and Dave Burt. Together they organized ParaVentures and later Parachuting Associates. They established a commercial sport parachuting center that also served as a base of operations for their varied professional parachuting projects. Among other activities, they developed major innovations in military use of the parachute in both North and South America. Since Hall was a geologist as well as a parachutist, it isn't surprising that he led a goldmining expedition that parachuted into an inaccessible region of the Sierra Madre Mountains. An air compressor and other necessary equipment were also parachuted in so they could work underwater in mountain streams and pools.

But their most famous project was the *Ripcord* television series, which

The buddy system of free-fall parachute training is a drastic departure from the traditional method of training. Instead of making several static-line jumps with immediate openings, the student begins with 60-second delayed free falls from 12,500 feet. Here Bud Kiesow (right) keeps a tight grip on his student, Major General Griffith, who made three "buddy" jumps. General Griffith was Deputy Inspector General for Safety for the U.S. Air Force. (Parachuting Associates, Inc.)

they established. The Ivan Tors production lasted only a couple of years in the early 1960's, but it put skydiving before millions of viewers for the first time. It was an airborne version of Tors' highly successful undersea adventure, *Sea Hunt*. Hall and Burt furnished the technical advice, jumpers, and equipment during the difficult stages and through the first year. Unfortunately, the plots were created by nonjumping writers rather than parachutists. The stories were so highly contrived that impossible situations developed. Amazingly, many of these "impossible" stunts actually were accomplished.

In addition to the television show, ParaVentures made numerous television shorts and scenes to be used in other TV shows as well as motion pictures. Commercials for television and short films on parachuting kept them active. They grew from a two-man operation until they had eleven full-time employees and had outgrown their shoestring operation. With the development of the para-scuba program and "buddy system" of free-fall training for military purposes, they decided to eliminate the sport parachuting operations and devote full time to professional parachuting services. With this new image, in 1963 they changed their organization to Parachuting Associates, Inc., with Burt and Hall exchanging positions as president and vice-president, and taking in a third, highly skilled professional, Bob Sinclair, as associate. Their Air Force training film *Passport to Safety* won numerous awards. Top professionals Arthur "Bud" Kiesow (with more than a thousand jumps to his credit) and Ralph Weekly (onetime paratrooper company commander) doubled as the Air Force pilots throughout the film. Exciting and dramatic motion picture footage was filmed in free fall with helmet-mounted cameras on the free-falling cameraman. Free-fall photographer Bob Sinclair took on this demanding specialty. They went on to film commercials of every type, including one for Lilt showing Carol Penrod setting her hair with curlers while in free fall, and one of another jumper loading Kodak's Instamatic camera and taking still shots of a fellow jumper. (Professional photographer/ jumper Carl Boenish did a similar Minolta commercial in the late 1970's.) Among the television shows in which their parachuting scenes were used were *Run for Your Life, 12 O'Clock High, Man from U.N.C.L.E., Voyage to the Bottom of the Sea, Kraft Theater*, and *Bob Hope's Chrysler Theater*. TV's Johnny Carson received his jump training and made his first jump, a 60-second delayed free fall, with Bob Sinclair as his "buddy-system" partner. It was filmed in free fall and aired on NBC's *Tonight Show* in July 1968.

Promotional jumps aren't new, particularly on television. Skydivers have been seen plugging a variety of products. In January 1980 an estimated television audience of 125 million viewers saw 22 skydivers jump into Super Bowl XIV. CBS wanted to have something a little different to introduce Super Sunday. And in promoting the Super Bowl, CBS also promoted skydiving. The actual jump was filmed in November at Pope Valley, California, by Rande Deluca and Tom Dunn. TV viewers saw a little over a minute of actual skydiving as the 22 jumpers built a free-fall "XIV" formation, a giant CBS "Eye" logo, the letter "A" for the American Football League, and the letter "N" for the National Football League. Based on the TV advertising cost per minute, USPA headquarters estimated skydiving received $550,000 worth of free promotion during the pregame and postgame shows.

The *Ripcord* TV show went on to "better" things (the second season was in color) and then to oblivion, at the hands of other professionals. The parachuting scenes were frequently concocted and unlikely, but everyone agreed they were different and interesting. If the actors and story had been as good as the parachuting photography and sequences, the show might have survived a little longer.

Parachuting Associates set the pace for excitement in the show when a "student," Bob Sinclair doubling, got tangled in his static line during a training drop. The hero, Dave Burt doubling, slid down the line, cut the static line, and they fell away. Then the hero opened his student's parachute before opening his own—not really as impossible as it may sound. It had actually happened in

Television's Johnny Carson gets an assist from professional parachutist Bob Sinclair. Johnny's first jump was a 60-second delayed free fall alongside Bob. This buddy system of training was developed by Parachuting Associates to train Air Force crewmen in free-fall techniques. (Parachuting Associates, Inc.)

October 1960, when George Van Roosmalen got tangled in his static line on his fourth student-training jump. His jumpmaster, Alfred Coxall, slid down the static line, which broke as he reached the student; Coxnall pulled the student's reserve ripcord and then, after falling clear of him, pulled his own.

The new cameramen and jumpers of the *Ripcord* TV show were pushed to do better things each week as the nonjumping writers came up with midair fist-fights, shoot-outs, and you-name-it. One of the most spectacular scenes was not planned in the script; they later wrote another show to use the unscheduled footage. Cliff Winters flew the hero's plane (Cessna 182) while Howard Curtis flew the villain's plane (L-13). The plot called for the hero, Lyle Cameron, to lower himself onto the tail of the villain's plane, where he would be able to control the villain's craft. The pilot of the hero's plane would then radio the villain, telling him to land or the hero would force the plane into the ground. They tried it several times with sandbags to see if Curtis could keep control with the extra weight on the plane's tail—he could. Cameras were rolling as the scene began as planned. Winters maneuvered in behind and above Curtis's plane, and Cameron prepared to lower himself. When the two planes were separated by only a dozen feet or so, Cameron lowered himself onto the plane below. Then everything went wrong.

Cameron's weight upset the control, causing the L-13 to nose-up and smash into the 182 above. Cameron let go of the plane as quickly as possible, but it was too late. Both planes began breaking up as Cameron fell clear. Both pilots were also highly skilled stunt parachutists, fortunately. Curtis fought for control of the plane, but as it rolled out of control, he cut all switches, released his seat belt, and bailed out—striking the wingstrut. He was dazed slightly, but quickly recovered, stabilized, and then pulled. He saw Cameron descending safely and watched his disabled plane smash into the middle of a tomato patch.

Winters wasn't having such an easy time with the 182. He had refused to wear a parachute because it hampered his movements. Director Leon Benson had insisted on it for this scene, however, so Winters wore a QAC type chute until after takeoff. Once airborne, he unsnapped it from its D-rings and tossed it on the floor behind him, leaving him with only the harness. When the midair collision came, the plane fell out of control and Winters knew he had to get out. He released his seat belt, clawed his way into the back of the tumbling plane, grabbed the chute by its carrying strap, and bailed out! While tumbling free through space (the crash came at 4,000 feet—26 seconds separated him from the earth), he struggled to snap the parachute back on his harness. Later, Curtis praised Winter's feat, comparing it to changing a tire while the car is still moving. Winters hooked up and opened in time to save his life. Shortly afterward, he was killed when his stunt plane's engine failed in inverted flight during a slow roll for an airshow crowd. Curtis died on a routine sport jump in September 1979.

Director of photography, Monroe Askins, filmed the entire smash-up and continued filming as long as there was anything to shoot. Because it cost them roughly $30,000, another script was written to make use of the special footage.

Another stunt called for a senator to leap from a disabled airplane, but without any parachute. The hero had to overtake him in free fall and catch him, and then they would come down on one chute. Leigh Hunt played the senator and dropped out wearing a gray flannel suit, complete with white shirt and tie. A 26-foot conical pack was sewn into the rear of his coat so it appeared he was chuteless. He wore no reserve, of course. Howard Curtis played the hero who made the catch. Hunt found that he fell too slowly without the added weight of his reserve so he had to wear skindiving weights. Swapping a reserve for lead is quite a switch!

Another time, Glenn White, playing the part of a girl, was to catch a box of cargo in midair and pull the broken static line to open the cargo chute. Lyle Cameron was the free-fall cameraman putting it on film. Glenn had trouble getting the box (full of sand), but finally succeeded. As Glenn opened, Lyle was in close filming the stunt, so he got a face full of Glenn's canopy. He went through it, remodifying White's Double-L canopy in the process.

In one episode Curtis played a dope-peddling villain whom hero Hunt catches in midair. The hero and the villain have a midair fist-fight and the hero knocks the villain unconscious. Then he takes a pistol out of the unconscious villain's pocket before pulling the villain's ripcord, then his own. Lyle Cameron

Professional jumping demands the ultimate in skill and daring. Here the good guy (Leigh Hunt) charges after the gun-toting bad guy (Howard Curtis) as cameraman Doyle Fields dangles from the wingstrut to film the scene for the now off-network television show *Ripcord*. (Ron Simmons, **Parachute** magazine)

captured every second of it on film. Ironically, after all the narrow escapes, Lyle broke his arm one peaceful day when he fell from his camera-perch in a tree! Don Molitor took over the camera.

Doyle Fields also did free-fall motion picture coverage, and Bob Buquor shot many exciting free-fall stills for publicity use. A few years later, with nearly a thousand safe jumps, Bob accidentally landed in the Pacific Ocean during some camera work and was drowned.

Certainly one of the closest calls of all came when the script called for the hero's main parachute to be ripped away so he had to resort to his reserve. Darrell Creighton did the camera work while standing on the top wing of a Stearman biplane piloted by Cameron. Howard Curtis almost became a dead hero as he gamely fought with the partial main (about a third had been removed to be sure it did not work) then deployed his reserve as the script called for. When the reserve malfunctioned along with the streaming main, he was in for some thrills. He pulled on lines and did everything possible to make it untangle and catch air. It finally caught and inflated inside the partial main—at roughly a hundred feet above ground.

In the summer of 1979 United Artists released the James Bond movie *Moonraker*. The opening scene involves a pitched battle in free fall between 007, who is pushed from the plane *without* a parachute, and the pilot, who has jumped from the plane *with* a parachute. Bond catches up with the pilot, gives him a few knuckle sandwiches, and takes the parachute for himself. Just when it looks like the hero has it made, the villain "Jaws" drops into view and another aerial battle takes place. Naturally Bond wins both battles.

Filmed at Pope Valley, California, the entire scene takes about two minutes on the screen but actually took five weeks and 83 jumps to accomplish. It also took some top professionals like Rande Deluca with a helmet-mounted 35-mm movie camera and wide-screen Panavision lenses. Peter Bottgenbach and Phil Pastuhov were also called upon for their combined jumper/cinematography talents. B. J. Worth was the "pilot" who lost his parachute to victorious 007, played by Jake Lombard. Ron Luginbill played the part of "Jaws."

These skydiving stuntmen not only had to be highly skilled in free-fall relative work, but also had to have a good understanding of photography. For continuity, each scene had to be shot from the same sun angle and have the same background orientation in order to make them fit together in the final product. So while chasing each other around the sky and engaging in mortal combat, they had to be sure Rande could film their action. For realism, the action had to fill the frame most of the time. A minimum distance was maintained between the combatants and the camera. To film close-ups of the tumbling and wrestling, Rande would hold on to them and then tumble through the sky with them. The result was heart-stopping action.

Garth Taggart jumping bat wings, doubles for Burt Lancaster in the feature film *Gypsy Moths*. Also starring in the film were Gene Hackman, Deborah Kerr, and Scott Wilson. (Carl Boenish)

The problems of filming such close-ups and actually becoming involved in the "fight" were many. The stuntman for actor Roger Moore's 007 had to look like Roger Moore. Jake Lombard did. That, plus his skill as a jumper, got him the job. Finding somebody the size of actor Richard Kiel (7 feet, 2 inches) to play the airborne "Jaws" was another problem, but 6-foot, 5-inch Ron Luginbill filled the bill. Once the actors and cameraman were selected, the equipment had to be designed. Canadian jumper Mike "Zeke" Zahar designed and built the "suit-rig" worn by the pilot and Bond. The business suit was velcroed together so that when the parachute was hand-deployed, the coat and pants would split allowing the Safety Flyer canopy to open. Flyers were used for both main and reserve since they pack up very small. An added problem: the fake movie parachute that Bond and the pilot fought over was actually a real danger to the stuntmen. Because their real parachutes were built into the suits of both jumpers, strapping on the fake parachute would make it impossible to open the real ones. So after wearing the fake parachute for Rande to photograph, the stuntman had to remove it before opening his real parachute. Jake put it on and took it off three times during a single jump while Rande filmed it all. During the last week of filming, Jake tore the cartilage in his knee and Don "Tweet" Caltvedt did the final scenes.

In the movie *The Nude Bomb*, Carl Boenish and Ray Cottingham filmed Kevin Donnelly performing a landing in a moving truck. Over a period of five days and approximately 25 jumps, they filmed the opening few minutes. The plot has Maxwell Smart in a large airplane full of people. Smart discovers these are all enemy agents and the chase is on. Smart dives out and the entire planeload of enemy agents dive out after him. They join up in a formation like a set of jaws, intent on closing in and crushing Smart. However, he does a front loop and drops below the converging forces just as they close. The lines smash into themselves and a battle ensues. Smart tracks out of the way and opens his parachute. One of the agents, who has also opened his parachute, realizes Smart is escaping and chases after him, catching up and docking his canopy above Smart's. The villain slides down Smart's lines intent on doing bodily harm to the hero. Smart cuts away from his main canopy and leaves the enemy agent with an empty parachute. Dangerously low to the ground, Smart opens his reserve parachute and lands in a fertilizer truck that just happens by at that precise split second. Keven made four jumps in a row to get the right shot, landing exactly on target on his fourth attempt. Ironically, these choice scenes were left on the cutting room floor.

Professional jumping requires risks and dangers that are avoidable in the sport of parachuting. However, the average person thinks of all parachute jumps as being about the same—a parachute jump is a parachute jump, they say. Rod Pack changed all that.

At 14,500 feet, Pack made his 534th parachute jump. The only thing unusual about this jump was the fact that he was intentionally making it without a parachute. He did it on New Years Day, 1965. Talk about starting the year off with a bang!

Pack got interested in sport jumping after seeing a movie short on sky-diving. He began jumping in October 1961 and made 306 jumps his first year, probably a record for a twelve-month period. A part-time movie stuntman, he got the idea for a stunt so spectacular that moviemakers would have to notice. Cliff Winters had made a parachute jump while in a straightjacket—he pulled the ripcord with his teeth. Somebody had commented that the only way to beat that was to jump without a parachute. Pack decided to do just that, but he wanted to live to tell about it.

He made his first jump with Bob Allen and his first hookup in relative work with Bob Buquor. He began practicing passing a standard 24-foot reserve parachute with Allen, but wore a main parachute as well. Each time he would catch up with Allen, take the reserve, and carefully snap it onto his special harness. After about a hundred practice jumps, Pack was ready for the real thing.

Kevin Donnelly makes a precision accuracy landing in a moving truck during the filming of the movie *The Nude Bomb*, starring Don Adams as Maxwell Smart. (Ray Cottingham)

Movie stuntman Rod Pack, seen here with his equipment, gained the attention he wanted when he became the first man to make an intentional parachute jump *without* a parachute. He picked one up from a friend on the way down and landed safely! (Bob Buquor)

His harness was constructed so the D-rings would stand out instead of lying flat against the webbing. As an additional safety precaution, his harness was fitted with an extra strap with a strong snap on the end. If anything should go wrong (the reserve had slipped out of their hands once during a practice jump) and he should be without the chute, he would try to hook onto Allen's harness and both come down on Allen's main chute. Finally they were ready for the try.

He secured some financial backing through television and periodical contracts and hired two top-notch free-fall cameramen who also happened to be close jump buddies of his. Doyle Fields handled the motion pictures while Bob Buquor rigged himself up for the still shots.

Although they had planned for 15,000 feet, Pack directed the pilot to start in on the final run at 14,600 feet because everybody was getting numb from the cold. Allen did the spotting and gave Pack the nod when all was set.

Robert H. Buquor, aircraft mechanic, pilot, and professional jumper, was considered by most people to be the best free-fall photographer of his time. Bob was chosen by Rod Pack to make free-fall shots of the chuteless jump and to act as backup man in case a midair rescue was necessary. With nearly 1,000 safe jumps, Bob accidentally landed in the Pacific Ocean during some camera work and drowned. The *Star Crest* award system was named in his honor. (Ralph White)

Pack signaled "go" and Allen dived out. Pack plunged out immediately after him, followed by cameramen Fields and Buquor.

To compensate for the lack of parachutes, Pack had weighted himself so he would fall at the same speed as during the practice jumps. As long as he was above Allen, he was still fairly sure of accomplishing the jump successfully—he could speed up his fall by pulling his arms and legs in or otherwise adjusting his body position. If he got below Allen he would be in trouble. He would have difficulty getting back up to Allen's level and Allen would have difficulty getting down to Pack's level. Allen was holding the reserve by the cloth handles at each end and could do little maneuvering without risking the chance of losing the chute. Pack ate up 4,000 feet carefully moving into position to take the chute. He could have done it in much less, but had ample time and did not want to rush things. He had 90 seconds from the time he left the plane until he would strike the ground. That was the "ample time."

He carefully moved in and got a firm grip on the heavy cloth handle on the top of the reserve. Allen hung on, afraid Pack didn't have a good grip. Pack nodded he had it, and Allen reluctantly released his grip. Instantly the reserve shot up over Pack's head, the 120 mph wind almost pulled it from his hand but he hung on, hoping the handle would not pull out. Allen hovered close at hand, ready to rush in and share his harness if Pack should lose his grip. Continuing to film the episode, Fields and Buquor moved in closer, ready to dart in for the midair rescue if Allen were to fail. Pack pulled the chute back down and positioned it under him as he fell face down in a head-high attitude. Although he could not hear the snap, he watched carefully and concentrated on snapping both D-rings securely. A sense of relief came over him as the last snap was in place and he knew he was safe—provided he didn't have a malfunction of his one and only chute.

He released his grip on the chute as he scanned the sky for his three fellow-jumpers and flared out in a stable position. Because there was no tie-down on the chute, it swung up on the D-rings and crashed into his face. He grabbed it and pushed it back down, tumbling momentarily. In an effort to push the reserve back into position his hand accidentally dragged the ripcord free and his chute caught air. He was not prepared for the opening shock, and his head and heels met somewhere behind him during the opening. He jubilantly drifted down for a soft landing in a plowed field.

He had done it! He had jumped without a parachute, picked one up on the way down, and landed safely . . . a stunt that might be duplicated, but not surpassed.

The repercussions of his stunt were inevitable. The Federal Aviation Administration required that a person wear *two* parachutes for any premeditated jump—he didn't even wear one! The jumper isn't the only one to hang for infractions of FAA regulations; the pilot shares the responsibility and pilot Harry Haynes was called on the carpet, too. U.S. Attorney Manuel Real filed a civil federal court suit against Pack asking $3,000 punitive damages and $4,000 against pilot Haynes. The legal outcome was never made public, but the representatives of the FAA made it clear they wanted to make an example of the jumper and the pilot to prevent any future stunts of that nature.

Rumors of what Pack's next stunt would be spread like wildfire—some had a touch of truth, some did not. Many said that the FAA had permanently grounded Pack from any future jumping from airplanes. So he began plans for parachuting from . . . an automobile? Yep. Nobody could prevent him from parachuting from an automobile. Plans called for him to drive the car out of the back of a C-130 some 15,000 feet above the Pacific Ocean. During the fall, explosive charges would blow the doors off. Then Pack would make a parachute jump *from the automobile.*

Actually, the FAA did not ground him at all, and he continued jumping until he broke his leg in three places (racing motorcycles, not parachuting). By the time he broke his leg, he had made an additional 64 parachute jumps since the chuteless drop some three months earlier.

Another stunt rumored to be in Pack's planning was dropping from the open cockpit of an inverted Stearman biplane, doing aerial maneuvers, and finally dropping back into the open seat once more. This would seem more feasible in a glider or jet—something without a propeller to chop him into mincemeat. This brings to mind an incident along similar lines.

In 1931 pilot Dimitrije Ljumovich's airplane seat belt broke at 8,000 feet as he was in the inverted position at the top of a proposed loop. Ljumovich dropped out, upside down, as his plane continued over in the arc to complete the loop in pilotless flight. At the bottom of the loop, the plane and Ljumovich met in midair, where the propeller neatly severed his leg. He opened his parachute, tore strips of cloth from his flying suit, and tied a tourniquet around the bleeding stump during descent. He landed on his one leg and not only lived, he lived to fly again—with a wooden leg.

But sooner or later it had to come: relative work between man and machine. Somebody had to accomplish a successful "hookup" with an airplane instead of with another jumper. In 1978 Hollywood stuntman Dar Robinson did it for NBC's TV special, *Super Stunt.* Three movie cameras were mounted on a Stearman biplane, piloted by Mike Dewey, and others were mounted on a helicopter cameraship. On the ground, huge Mitchel cameras with telephoto lenses filmed the action. But for the really sensational close-ups, top professional cameraman and skydiver Ray Cottingham was called in to free-fall along with Robinson, filming with both still and motion picture cameras.

Several trial runs were made by Dewey, experimenting with various sized drogue chutes in an effort to find the right combination. Careful calculations by Dewey, Robinson, and aeronautical project engineer Ed Drumheller eventually produced the desired results. They tried a 6-foot drogue chute first, but the rate of descent of the Stearman in a vertical dive was too fast. A 9-foot drogue was too fast still. With a 12-foot drogue on a 150-foot bridle line, calculations indicated they would have the right combination, and Robinson went aloft in a separate plane to give it a try. The rate of fall was slower than previous attempts but still too fast—roughly 140 mph. Robinson managed to catch the Stearman by diving all the way from 12,500 down to 5,500 feet, but control was very difficult at this speed. Suddenly the bridle cord broke, and the biplane shot ahead. Dewey quickly pulled out of the dive, and Robinson opened his parachute.

At 7,000 feet, Dar Robinson catches up with the Stearman plane with which he has been doing relative work and makes contact prior to climbing aboard. The entire sequence was filmed for the NBC-TV special *Super Stunt*. Skydiver-photographer Ray Cottingham and stuntman Robinson exited two different planes at 11,500 feet as the Stearman deployed a drogue chute and nosed over into a dive. (Ray Cottingham)

On the ground they did some more figuring. The problem with the broken bridle cord was solved and a second attempt was made. This time the cord held and Robinson got closer, but still the speeds were too great, and it was obvious they would have to go to an even larger drogue. For attempt number three, they went to a 16-foot drogue chute on a 200-foot bridle line. At 12,500 feet Dewey deployed the 16-foot drogue and immediately the Stearman pitched over into a vertical dive. Robinson dived out of the jump plane at 12,500 feet when he saw the drogue deploy. At 8,000 feet Robinson caught up and quickly moved into the contact position on the wing, where nylon webbing had been stretched between the wing brace wires. Once he had a secure grip and was firmly in place on the wing, Dewey pulled the nose of the Stearman up and released the drogue. They landed with Robinson on the wing. Now that they had the right combination, they had to do it all again for the cameras.

This "camera" jump—number four—was almost Robinson's last. With

Robinson and free-fall cameraman Cottingham both in the Cessna jump plane, the added weight caused it to stall slightly just as the two planes were in position at 12,500 feet. Dewey pulled the drogue and nosed the Stearman over in a dive. Robinson dived out of the Cessna 182, with Cottingham right behind filming the action. At about 5,000 feet, time and altitude were running out, when Robinson made a fast approach and missed the contact point on the wing. Instead, he went under the wing, bounced off the wheel, and then dived past the spinning propeller with inches to spare. Suddenly roles were reversed. Now he was on his back in *front* of the plane, looking up into the terrifying propeller closing down on him! He quickly rolled over into a dive and escaped by tracking out of the plane's path.

Back on the ground they critiqued the last jump and made a few revisions for number five. Because of the heat of the day, two jump planes were used and the jump altitude lowered to 11,500 feet. This time everything went perfectly with Robinson exiting one plane and Cottingham exiting another. The contact was made smoothly at 7,000 feet with all cameras filming man and machine doing relative work. It was decided that another jump for the cameras was needed for additional footage of the free fall down to the point of contact. As a safety precaution, nylon webbing was criss-crossed between the landing gear legs and from the left gear leg out to the wingtip. The camera jump went off perfectly as Cottingham filmed Robinson's free fall from 12,500 feet all the way to point of contact.

Later it was decided that one final jump for the cameras should be made, as "insurance." However, this "insurance" jump for the cameras nearly cost Robinson his life. Both Robinson and Cottingham had perfect exits, and all went as planned as Robinson caught up with the Stearman and climbed aboard the wing at 6,000 feet. As Dewey turned the plane downwind at 500 feet for the landing with Robinson crouched on the wing, he was horrified to see Robinson's pilot chute starting to creep out of his backpack. If the pilot chute caught air at this point, Robinson would be yanked through the tail brace wires, coming out on the other side in an assortment of disassembled pieces. Dewey grabbed the back of the pack and attracted Robinson's attention. When Robinson saw what was happening, he grabbed the pilot chute cord and signaled for Dewey to land as quickly as possible. The Stearman touched down with Robinson hanging onto the wing with one hand and his pilot chute with the other. Robinson had not only succeeded in doing "relative work" with the Stearman, but he had been successful in climbing aboard the diving plane four times.

Johnny Findley of Bloomington, Indiana, is only a part-time professional jumper, but his experiences are typical. This writer "trained" Johnny back in pre-PCA basic safety rules days and sent him aloft in a two-place plane to spot for himself and make a free fall. He was cautioned simply to get clear of the plane and pull; we would concentrate on stable delay later—say on the second or third jump! Johnny jumped from 2,500 feet, did a beautiful stable delay of ten seconds, and opened. He experienced a minor malfunction of his main canopy (flat circular, no sleeve or bag) but elected to ride it into the ground rather than inconvenience his instructor by opening the reserve.

An expert at both scuba diving and spelunking, Johnny frequently combines the two by exploring underwater caves. His daring is excelled only by his limitless energy. It is not uncommon for him to spend the entire night exploring caves (he doesn't want to waste the daylight) and the entire day parachuting, flying, scuba diving, or shooting the rapids of a flooded mountain stream.

When Johnny found that he could make money by jumping out of airplanes, he turned professional—on his second or third jump. Promoters who advertise and publicize a jump usually expect to see a jump made regardless of the weather, so most parachutists who contract for an exhibition jump go ahead and make it even at the risk of serious injury. Unfortunately, Johnny is no exception.

He had had seven years' experience when he prepared for three "pay" jumps on Armed Forces Day. He knew the winds were too high, but he wouldn't cancel out. The first two downwind landings were rough. The third was a typical "crash and burn" type landing that put him in the hospital for half a year, wearing plaster pants up to his armpits. He had to come in downwind to clear some obstacles, and just as he was about to land, a gust of wind caught his canopy and led him into the ground—both hitting about the same time. Winds are the greatest threat to jumpers, but the spectators don't know that.

The professional parachutist can find himself doing some very strange things, celebrating holidays and promoting special events and products. Chris Wentzel, an excellent aerial photographer as well as a skydiver, has parachuted into football stadiums to deliver the football and into a baseball stadium dressed as a Baltimore Oriole. Another time he jumped into a baseball stadium to deliver five diamond rings for "Ladies Diamond Ring Day." He has parachuted onto a 15 by 30 foot barge in the middle of Baltimore's Inner Harbor and even delivered a live crab by parachute for the National Hard Crab Derby. Once he dressed up in a complete lacrosse outfit, including stick, and parachuted into the College All-Stars Lacrosse Championships at night! Like many skydivers, Chris is also active in other "unusual" adventures like spelunking and scuba diving. His motion pictures and still photographs have been seen by millions. (He even took the jacket photo for this book.)

Every jumper who has done very many professional jumps experiences unique situations that cannot be anticipated. I remember making an exhibition jump with my partner, Jim Thompson. We were descending into a county fair one Saturday afternoon when blasting commenced in the quarry adjoining the

Santa Claus jumps such as this one by Jim Wilkins are always popular with the kids, but helicopters are usually more reliable for delivering Santa to the right place at the right time. (Ray Cottingham)

vacant field. We hung helplessly like clay pigeons, waiting to be literally shot out of the saddle by flying rocks. Another time, I was descending into an extremely tight area in front of the outdoor stage facing the grandstand at a county fair. A sudden and violent squall swept the area. I looked down to see the backdrop and parts of the stage blow away along with some of the tents. Although I had hit the target on the first jump, on this one I hitchhiked back from nearly a mile downwind of the fairgrounds.

Although the Santa Claus jumps are becoming less frequent—coming in by helicopter is more positive—they still thrill the kids and parents alike. Unfortunately, several deaths have occurred during Santa Claus jumps. Because of the bad weather over most of the country during the winter, "Santas" parachuting in have been blown into rivers and drowned, or into power lines and electrocuted.

Even if Santa Claus doesn't drift off into the surrounding countryside or get killed, he may break his ankle like Charles Barnes did at Panama City, Florida. The children's shouts of glee gave way to murmurs of concern as Santa moaned and groaned and writhed on the ground, holding his ankle. A stand-in Santa slipped under the parachute's folds with Barnes and switched into the Santa costume. The stand-in Santa walked away with all the children trotting happily after him. When most of the children were gone, ambulance attendants dragged Barnes out from under the parachute and took him to the hospital for treatment.

Santa jumps go back as far as December 1912, when a Captain Penfold arranged the jump with a chocolate company. Wearing the outfit of "Father Christmas," he ascended to 3,000 feet in a balloon and floated down in a parachute. When he landed, he passed out chocolate candy to the local children.

Because there are so many enthusiastic sport jumpers who are willing to jump for glory instead of money, the professional parachutist frequently finds himself losing out at airshows, county fairs, and other special celebrations. Some years ago a jumper could expect to make no less than $100 per jump—a jump-and-pull from 2,500 feet. But as more and more skilled jumpers became available, the price decreased and the performance improved (good old American competition?). Without an ironclad contract, the professional jumper could expect to be put out of the running by local jump clubs or individuals who would jump for much less—frequently for cost of the plane rental only. Instead of a jump-and-pull from 2,500 feet, the sponsor could now expect (and get) multiple jumps with different colored smoke from the jump plane and jumpers, and pinpoint accuracy in multicolored, specially manufactured sport parachutes—all for only the cost of gas and oil for the jump plane!

If somebody were to start a book of parachuting records, the top-paying jump would probably be the one made by skyjacker "D. B. Cooper."

In November 1971 a man calling himself Dan Cooper (the name was mistakenly picked up as D. B. Cooper, and that name stuck) bought a ticket in Portland, Oregon, for the short hop to Seattle, Washington. En route aboard the Northwest Orient Boeing 727 jetliner, he claimed to have a bomb and demanded $200,000 and four parachutes. The plane circled for two and a half hours while the money and parachutes were obtained.

At Seattle, the money and parachutes were put aboard and Cooper released the passengers and two of the three stewardesses. The pilot was ordered to fly the plane to Reno, Nevada, as slowly as possible. By now darkness had set in and the plane took off into the night without any visible lights, gear and flaps down. The stewardess was ordered into the forward cabin with the flight crew and told to keep the door locked until they reached Reno.

Shortly after takeoff, the pilot received a signal on his instruments that indicated the rear exit door had been opened in flight. Upon reaching Reno it was discovered that Cooper, two of the four parachutes, and the money were no longer aboard the aircraft. Everything else is speculation.

The many questions that surround the case are as intriguing as the incident itself. Why did he ask for only $200,000 when he could have asked for much more? Was it to be a large enough figure to be worthwhile, yet small

In 1980 the smoke jumpers adopted the 32-foot XP-5 parachute, which has mesh-covered openings that assure positive deployment and steerability, yet descend more slowly than older, less maneuverable parachutes of the past. (U.S. Forest Service)

enough to be easily obtained in a short time? Why two sets of parachutes? Was he going to take a hostage with him or was he only bluffing to make the authorities think so? They would be inclined to furnish airworthy parachutes if they thought a hostage would also be jumping. Was it beginner's luck or careful planning that he made his escape flight after darkness when it would be impossible to see him jump out? Did he jump out immediately after opening the rear exit, or did he stay in the plane for some time before his escape? Since he knew how to open the rear exit on a 727 in flight, and had given the pilot very precise instructions on how and where to fly the aircraft, was he also a pilot or mechanic familiar with a 727's operation?

Most intriguing of all, was he a parachutist? At this time, nobody had ever bailed out of a 727. Even flying "slow," the 727 would be moving about 200 mph. Terminal velocity—the normal opening speed in a sport jump—is about 120 mph. Would an experienced parachutist leap into a 200 mph windblast wearing just any old parachute the FBI chose to give him? In this case, the parachute was a low-speed (150 mph maximum), 28-foot flat circular surplus parachute without any deployment device. That means he decelerated from 200 mph to zero in approximately one second. (Yet at that time there were sport parachutes that could easily have functioned safely at that speed.) When last seen by the stewardess, Cooper was dressed in a dark business suit with low-cut dress shoes. The force of the opening would have been enough to knock his shoes off and probably knock him unconscious. Very likely it would have been hard enough to break his back or neck. Any money he carried, even tied to him, would have been ripped away during the opening shock. But assuming he and his parachute survived the opening shock, he would have been left dangling in freezing rain and snow at 10,000 feet.

During the next five to ten minutes of descent (depending on how much of his parachute was destroyed by the opening shock and the height of the terrain on which he landed) he would be subjected to subzero temperatures and wind gusts up to 70 mph. Barefoot, broke, injured, and freezing, he would descend

Professional jumping often requires special equipment or aircraft. When the author had to make three successive water jumps during an afternoon water show, he called on his friend and fellow pilot D. C. Lovelace. Here, with Lovelace at the controls of his floatplane, the author makes a dry-run test drop. (George Green)

along with the freezing rain and snow. To those of us who have made night jumps, landing in total darkness on a clear drop zone is exciting. But if Cooper was conscious enough to be aware of his situation, it would have been terrifying. Somewhere below him in the icy darkness was extremely rough terrain—lakes, rivers, rocks, and trees.

Is it possible that he knew so little about jumping that he would ask for parachutes without being specific in his demand? Steve Snyder's *Para-Plane* and Pioneer's *Volplane* were a couple of the high-performance parachutes available back then as well as the ever-popular *Para-Commander*. These chutes have deployment devices to slow the opening to a tolerable level and performance characteristics to give maximum control and maneuverability. Why didn't Cooper ask for one of these? And why was he in a business suit instead of more suitable attire? If he didn't know more than it appears he knew about parachutes, possibly he didn't know any more about parachute jumping either. Surely he wasn't making his first parachute jump out of a jetliner flying 200 mph in a snowstorm at night. This sort of thing would be attempted only by an experienced expert, wouldn't it? The questions go on.

Nobody has seen or heard of Cooper since the stewardess left him alone in the passenger compartment and locked herself in the cockpit with the crew. However, on February 10, 1980, some of the marked money was found, buried

USPA Executive Director Bill Ottley drops away from an inverted biplane piloted by the late Dr. Ed Fitch, a former USPA director. Parachuting demonstrations have always been an important part of any airshow. (Carl Boenish)

Skydiver J. C. Harrison prepares to exit a PT-19 over Yolo, California, during a parachuting demonstration. (Carl Boenish)

in the sand along the shores of the Columbia River not far from Portland. The twelve weathered stacks of marked $20 bills were still bound by rubber bands as originally packaged. Because of the deteriorated condition of the bills, which were crumbling along the edges, the exact amount could not be determined, but the serial numbers matched. The only known unsolved skyjacking remains unsolved. Dead or alive, "D. B. Cooper" has become a folk hero. T-shirts have been printed: "D. B. Cooper, Where Are You?" A song has been written about him, a Washington town has an annual "D. B. Cooper Day," and a movie has been made about him. No matter how you figure it, this remains the most expensive jump made—costing the airline $200,000 and probably costing Cooper his life.

Professional jumping calls for many demands, few more demanding than the one done by Rick Sylvester for a James Bond movie back in 1972. He skied off the top of El Capitan, the 3,000-foot monolith in Yosemite National Park, California. The momentum of his skis carried him far enough away from the face of the cliff to open his delta-shaped, slotted canopy after dropping 1,500 feet. From there he glided unceremoniously into a pine tree landing.

Sylvester was more experienced in skiing than in skydiving. This was only his 55th jump, which included an unintentional backflip as he left the snow ramp he and his eight companions had built the night before. To avoid the park authorities, they had been secretly lifted to the top of El Capitan by a helicopter. Sylvester, a professional skier and an excellent mountain climber, had once worked for the mountaineering school at Yosemite and had climbed El Capitan. He had also worked as a ski instructor at nearby Badger Pass. Every phase of the stunt had been carefully planned. He had made a couple of jumps with dummy skis to be sure the special pull rings for his bindings would work properly to release the skis before opening his chute. Such careful planning was not always the case. Back in 1966, two men jumped from the monolith with conventional round canopies in bad weather conditions; both were seriously injured.

The park has attracted hang glider enthusiasts for a number of years and legal flights have been made with the permission of the park officials. Permits are issued for mountain climbing as well as for hang gliding. Sooner or later, somebody would assert the equal rights for skydivers to parachute from El Capitan, not as Sylvester's one-time stunt but as an ongoing activity. Carl Boenish took up the cause. He gathered a small army of expert parachutists to prove it could be done safely and to assert every qualified skydiver's right to engage in cliff jumping. There was no law against jumping off a mountain in the park, although eventually Boenish and his cliff jumpers were charged with violating a federal law which bars "delivery by air of a person by parachute or other means without the prior written permission of the superintendent" of the park. They were hardly delivered by air because they were already in the park at the time they jumped. Here's how it happened.

In the summer of 1978, after months of careful planning and preparations, Carl Boenish and a dozen or so diehard, dedicated individualists made a pact to jump from El Capitan. Not only would they jump, they would carefully document the jumps on film. A few weeks before the jumps, planned for August, Carl and his crew built a 60-pound ladder that would be projected out over the face of the cliff and afford a perch from which to film the jumpers. The disassembled ladder, guywires, and other paraphernalia were taken up a week before the jumps and stashed under an outcrop at the top of El Capitan. They had painted everything black to make it as inconspicuous as possible. In August, sixteen people made the first trip to the top for jumps. They went prepared to spend a number of days, if necessary, to study the winds and determine the best jump conditions. The weight factor was so critical that they even resorted to cutting the handles off their toothbrushes.

Although the jumpers felt what they were doing was right and didn't break any existing laws, they also decided to use utmost discretion and avoid

Cliff jumper David Blattel is captured by a rear-facing camera mounted on fellow cliff jumper Carl Boenish, as the two plunge over the face of El Capitan in Yosemite National Park. They free-fell 1,000 feet before hand-deploying their pilot chutes and landing safely. (Carl Boenish)

Carl Boenish, without benefit of a parachute, balances on the end of a pole more than half a mile above the ground to get the correct angle for filming Mike Sheerin's skydive off El Capitan in Yosemite National Park. (Carl Boenish)

any confrontation with the authorities. Early in the morning the winds were calm, the sunlight was perfect, and conditions were excellent. With cameras (both still and motion) coordinated by radio communications from a dozen vantage points, the first jumper, Kent Lane, took a running start and dived over the ledge. He tracked out for several seconds before opening his square parachute and making a gentle standup landing precisely where planned. Tom Start was next, followed by world champion Mike Sheerin. Ken Gosslin was number four. Everything went perfectly. That weekend they gathered to view the films and get some ideas for improving the coverage of the next jumps.

A couple of weeks later, on September 9, six more jumps were made. This time it was decided to make the jumps in pairs rather than individually. The jumpers wore forward-facing and rear-facing cameras to film each other in free fall, in addition to the several stationary cameras filming from various points around the mountain. Again Kent Lane led off, with Mike Sheerin right behind him. Next Tom Start and Joe Morgan took the plunge. Carl Boenish and Dave Blattel were the last pair to leave, but before their jump they climbed down to recover a few last items from the outcrop just below the exit point.

As they climbed back onto the top, they discovered that a couple of foreign, non-English speaking hikers had arrived. The hikers saw Carl and Dave reach the top, wearing what appeared to be mountain climbers' apparel and packs. The foreigners were thrilled to witness what they thought were two climbers reaching the top of the 3,000-foot cliff. Both Carl and Dave tried to explain what was going on but could not make themselves understood. Finally they gave up, turned and prepared for their takeoff run. Carl was first, with

Having stashed some of their gear under the outcropping, Carl Boenish and David Blattel climbed back on top. Two foreign hikers came by at the precise moment that Boenish and Blattel reached the top and mistook them for mountain climbers. Unable to communicate their intentions, the two skydivers smiled and waved before turning and taking the flying leap off the cliff, pictured here. (Carl Boenish)

Dave right behind him. As incredible as the free-fall cliff-jumping photographs were, all of us would love to have had a picture of the expressions on the faces of the hikers! Somewhere in this world are two hikers telling a wild story of two mountain climbers who had no more than reached the top of the cliff when they turned and leaped off it!

Since the first jumps had gone so perfectly with no static from the park rangers (actually, none saw them three weeks earlier when they jumped), the elated cliff jumpers made no attempt to conceal themselves or evade the authorities. But word leaked out the night before the second jumps, and a crowd of more than 200 people were gathered looking up at the top of El Capitan that morning. Among the 200 were a couple of rangers, curious about what the crowd was doing. Dave Blattel landed less than 50 feet from a ranger on horseback, and the questions began. Eventually the jumpers were cited and the legal hassles started. Later the park service issued permits based on safety recommendations from USPA; then later still the permits were withdrawn. At this

Exhibition parachuting requires both nerve and skill. Dropping into a baseball stadium, these Golden Knights of the U.S. Army Parachute Team score another one for the recruiting service. (**Milwaukee Journal** Photo)

writing, cliff jumping at Yosemite is still an unsettled question. USPA and the ten original cliff jumpers are pushing for regulated, safe cliff jumping as opposed to unregulated, outlaw-type jumping.

Very few of the thousands of free-fall parachutists in the United States can make a living solely by parachuting from airplanes. Professional stuntmen jumping for movies or television specials do very well, but the opportunities are obviously limited. However, as the sport grows, more and more "money meets" are held. Instead of winning a ten-dollar trophy, a contestant might win valuable equipment or a cash prize.

One of the oldest continuously operating competition circuits in the country is the Mid-Eastern Parachute Association, which was organized in 1963. The nonprofit organization consists of parachute clubs in New York, New Jersey,

Pennsylvania, Delaware, Maryland, and Virginia. Holding three accuracy competitions yearly, with events for both novice and expert, MEPA awards money and trophies to the winners. The scores for all three meets are totaled and an annual individual and team champion are declared. The top ten finishers for the year are awarded a lucite block with the MEPA insignia suspended in it. There are two perpetual trophies that go to the first-place individual and first-place team. They have their names engraved on the trophies and keep them until new champions are declared the following year. The 1979 MEPA champion was Dave Waight, a member of the Maytown (Pennsylvania) Skydiving Club and a USPA Eastern Conference Director. At the annual MEPA banquet he was awarded a new *XL CLOUD*, presented by Elek Puskas, president of Para-Flite, Inc., a leading manufacturer of sport parachuting equipment. Former USPA national director Len Potts and current USPA executive director Bill Ottley were two of those who originated MEPA. Other members or alumni include Frank Paynter, Stan Hicks, Curt Curtis, Al King, Joe Imbriaco, and Clayton Schoepple, who was 1969 National Champion and 1972 World Champion. Bill Briedis, a two-time MEPA Champion, was also the 1974 Para-Ski Champion.

Like the golf or the tennis pro, the parachuting pro can follow the circuit and pick up money, equipment, and other prizes. A number of "money meets" have awarded first prizes of $1,000 or more, but these meets are still a long way from offering the winnings available to tennis and golf professionals. Professional jumping, at least on a part-time basis, is within the grasp of the weekend sport jumper, but presently the opportunities to make a decent living in parachuting appear to be limited to those who operate professional jump centers or design and build parachuting equipment.

MILITARY

Before leaving the general area of exhibition-demonstration-professional jumping, special mention should be made of the various military teams. Although there are teams, clubs, and individuals representing virtually every branch of our military services, the United States Army Parachute Team must be recognized as the leader. Largely through the efforts of Jacques Istel, free-fall parachuting gained both respectability and acceptance by the military.

The Army was the first to not only allow, but actually encourage, free-fall parachuting activities. In April 1958 it issued authorization and got a head start on the other services. The Navy followed in September 1960 with approval of the United States Navy Parachute Exhibition Team, which became "The Chuting Stars." However, it wasn't until January 1962 that the Navy issued SECNAV Instruction 1700.6C, which actually authorized and encouraged participation of Navy and Marine Corps personnel in free-fall parachuting.

In 1959 Istel had managed to get through to General Curtis LeMay and sold the idea of sport parachuting to the Air Force. Shortly after, a message went out to all commands stating that the local base commander could authorize his men to jump, provided they were a club sanctioned by PCA. The only trouble was that the majority of base commanders would not do so. Since they had a choice, they took the status quo attitude. In 1962 the U.S. Air Force in Europe published regulation 215-3, which opened the door wider and allowed many Air Force clubs to develop. Colonel Don R. Strobaugh (the Air Force's jumpingest officer with more than 3,200 jumps) originated and led the U.S. Air Force Parachute Demonstration Team in Europe. Known as the "Blue Masters," they traveled to thirteen countries in Europe and the Near East, jumping before such heads of state as King Constantine of Greece and the Shah of Iran. A few years later an unfortunate accident resulted in the disbanding of the Blue Masters team. In 1964 a PCA-backed effort to get parachuting approved for Air Force personnel without their base commander's permission was submitted and officially rejected. However, through the diligent work of a handful of dedicated Air Force men, sport parachuting was added to the curriculum of the Air Force Academy.

In 1964 Major John Garrity, Captain Craig Elliot, Sergeant James Howell, and Sergeant Morton Freedman were temporarily assigned to the Academy to set up a cadet parachute club, train jumpmasters, and establish operating procedures. Later, Major Garrity, Sergeant Freedman, and Sergeant Vernon Morgan were assigned on permanent basis to conduct two credit-earning courses. Although the cadet could earn semester hours, the course was strictly voluntary.

Although the Air Force does not at this writing have a full-time demonstration parachute team, some of the combat control teams at various Air Force bases perform for public functions. Also, the U.S. Air Force Academy has a team, "Wings of Blue," that gives public demonstrations. Four parachuting courses are included in the curriculum at the Academy.

There are other Air Force parachutists—all relatively small groups when compared with the Army's thousands—and all are specialists in their trade. The Air Rescue Service is one of the oldest groups. With their motto, "That Others May Live," these paramedics and pararescue crews circle the globe, performing yeoman service by snatching people back from the grave. Victims of air crashes, boat sinkings, floods, earthquakes, and other natural or man-made disasters represent some of those saved by the pararescue team. These hardy jumpers are trained medical technicians, ready to parachute into all types of situations to sustain life.

Space doesn't permit extensive coverage of this vital work or of the many miracles performed by these men, but without any doubt, the pararescue

Wings of Blue, the United States Air Force Academy parachute team, is composed of cadet parachutists. Since the team was organized in 1966, the cadets have competed annually in the National Collegiate Parachuting League and scored highly. (U.S. Air Force Academy)

jumpers are among the most skilled professionals of any service. With the advent of the space age the role of the pararescue team increased to include scuba training. Teams of parascuba men are ready to parachute into any waters to recover astronauts who, through some emergency situation, are forced down outside the prime recovery areas where Navy frogmen teams normally come in by helicopter to perform this function.

Another relatively small group of Air Force parachutists is the Combat Control team. These men are air traffic controllers who have the unpleasant job of jumping in ahead of the main airborne troops. Once on the ground, they set up drop zone and landing zone aids, direct paradrops of men and equipment, and control the air traffic in and out of the fighting area. Often found side by side with the combat controllers are the combat weather teams, whose mission is to assist in the airborne invasion with up-to-date meteorological data.

There may even be a 1,500-mph jet jockey jumping in the same load with his army paratroop friends. His unique role is to direct air strikes in support of

Yolande Hustinx steers her Papillon toward the drop zone. This French version of Pioneer's Para-Commander is still a highly respected parachute. (Ray Cottingham)

the ground troops. Through his Forward Air Controller's flying and jump training, he knows both the Army and Air Force problems, limitations, and capabilities, and thereby can give vital air strike assistance to the ground forces.

And there are others—each a small but vital unit: the Air Force Intelligence teams, survival technicians, Air Force liaison officers with the Army airborne units, and the Air Commandos (the counterinsurgency unit).

When the Army approved and encouraged parachuting for sport in 1958, clubs were quickly formed at Fort Campbell, Kentucky, and Fort Bragg, North Carolina, training bases of the Army airborne troops. Although the United States Army Parachute Team (USAPT) based at Fort Bragg has been instrumental in developing and testing new equipment and techniques, its main function has been one of public relations.

In February 1964 the team was authorized forty-two enlisted men and seven officers plus three officer-pilots and two flight engineers. They were divided into three teams: the competition team, the black demonstration team, and the gold demonstration team. Research and testing are conducted by parachutists from any of the three teams. Selection to the USAPT is a feather in the cap of any parachutist because qualifications are high and the number who can be accepted are few; vacancies are filled as each member completes his tour of duty with the team. For several years, at every major international parachute competition, the American team was dominated by members of the U.S. Army Parachute Team and, even before the team was officially formed, by members of the airborne.

The Navy's original "Chuting Stars" demonstration team was established in Pensacola, Florida, in the early 1960's, and a few years later was lost in a budget cut. Then, in the mid-1970's the Navy established a new "Chuting Stars" demonstration team on the East Coast at Norfolk, Virginia. At the same time, they set up a West Coast demonstration team at Coronado, California, called the "Leap Frogs." Getting on either team isn't easy. Candidates must first be members of the Navy's elite Underwater Demolition Team (UDT or Frogmen, as they are more commonly known) or SEAL team (Sea, Air, Land—sort of a Green Beret of the Navy). In addition to being a member of UDT or SEAL, candidates must be experienced free-fall parachutists before being accepted on the team. Other factors considered are the candidate's overall parachute knowledge, safety consciousness on the ground and in the air, and ability to project a favorable image to the general public during demonstrations. Professionalism in parachuting demonstrations was summed up well by Chief Bill Goines of the Chuting Stars when he said, "We have more than our lives (at stake), we have our reputations." The teams are attached to Naval Recruiting Command.

Early competition jumpers from the Army, such as Loy Brydon, Danny Byard, and Curt Hughes, were instrumental in designing, testing, and manufacturing parachutes with modifications of much higher performance than the blank gore parachute. Forming a company called Capital Parachuting Enterprises, the three designed and hold patents on the Double-L, Single-T, Double-T, and TU modifications. These were the winning chutes at every major parachute competition until the development of sport chutes like the Para-Commander and Cross-Bow. Although the TU modification had a high rate of descent, it also had the most forward speed. Dead-center landings were difficult, but men like Dick Fortenberry and Loy Brydon made them look easy. This modification was very unforgiving of mistakes, however, and many a jumper has been wiped out temporarily by turning too close to the ground.

The many military parachuting activities are so diversified, it is difficult to adequately discuss each one individually. Certainly the uses of the parachute by the Special Forces (Green Beret) in unconventional warfare must be briefly mentioned. They have held the major role in the development of project HALO (High Altitude–Low Opening).

The United States Navy demonstration team, Chuting Stars, builds a star high over one of the many cities for which they performed. Unlike sport jumps that are made over cleared drop zones, demonstration jumps are often made over congested locations. (U.S. Navy)

Training for HALO operations, two of the Army's Special Forces members begin their two-minute free fall. The Air Force and Navy also have training in HALO techniques. Contrast this with the traditional mass drops from low-flying troop carriers. (U.S. Army)

The conventional way of getting airborne troops into a given area is by helicopter or by large troop-carriers. Both must come in over the enemy territory at low altitude and they make enough noise to wake the dead. In the parachute operations from troop carriers, hundreds of airborne troops are dumped into the sky. Parachutes are automatically opened by static lines at a thousand feet or so and the soldier drifts down, completely at the mercy of the enemy's ground fire—and there is enemy fire if there is an enemy within five miles of the drop zone. An enemy would have to be deaf not to hear the planes at such a low altitude and would have to be blind not to see the sky darkened by hundreds of parachutes. If the planes come in over the territory at a higher altitude, the jumpers are simply drifting down that much longer and can drift that much farther from the intended drop zone. Project HALO eliminates these hazards.

Highly specialized teams—experienced free-fall parachutists expert in

Mass drops of airborne troops are becoming a thing of the past as helicopter assaults are more suitable to modern warfare. For special, behind-the-line guerrilla operations, HALO specialists are called in. (U.S. Air Force)

demolitions, communications, weapons or medicine—exit a relatively small, single-engine plane flying some 20,000 feet above their objective. The plane is too high to be heard or seen. Carrying large quantities of explosives and other necessary equipment, the team free-falls, using skydiving techniques to maintain stability and to glide to the proper opening point, down to very low altitudes where they deploy the chutes and land immediately. Unless an enemy is almost on the landing spot of the individual HALO jumper, the jump will go undetected.

A more recent innovation to this concept is project STAND-OFF, in which the team members open their parachutes immediately upon exit. Flying their ram-air inflated canopies into a tight formation, the entire team descends from high altitude. Several highly specialized teams may be dropped into the area at one time, each with some specific objective such as a bridge, dam, power plant, or other vital facility. A dozen skilled specialists, whose presence is unknown to the enemy, can do more damage with less risk than several hundred regular paratroopers who have alerted the entire countryside with a traditional mass drop.

This doesn't mean that there are not still occasions when sheer masses are necessary, of course, but for special guerrilla-type assignments, the HALO and STAND-OFF specialists are the answer. The Navy's SEAL teams specialize in unconventional warfare which also includes parachuting activities.

SMOKE JUMPERS

Although the concept of fighting an enemy through the use of aerial drops of men and supplies goes back to Ben Franklin, the practical aspects of this type of warfare were actually ironed out by a handful of determined and dedicated men who adopted the idea to fight fires, not wars.

From shortly after World War I until 1939 there had been some meager attempts to use aircraft both for spotting fires and for bombing them with water and chemicals. In 1939 the bombing experiments were given up in favor of experimenting with dropping firefighters, as well as equipment, by parachute. The Eagle Parachute Company of Lancaster, Pennsylvania, got the contract to furnish the equipment and jumpers for the experiment. Their training outfit consisted of an Eagle 30-foot main backpack chute and a 27-foot reserve chute. Eagle also manufactured a felt-padded suit that would protect the jumper from tree landings or unusually rough terrain. Frank M. Derry was in charge of the small group of professional jumpers who participated. In 1942 Derry designed the Derry Slot steerable canopy, which was used for many years in the Forest Service.

The experiment proved that aerial firefighters, smoke jumpers, could effectively reduce loss of valuable forests. In the first year of operations the smoke jumpers earned their keep by saving an estimated $30,000 worth of timberland. Watching the training and operations were four Army staff officers.

Demonstration jumps put even the best skydiver to the test once in a while. Here Carl Boenish tries to avoid both electrocution and a surging crowd at Van Nuys Airport. (Carl Boenish)

One officer was Major William Cary Lee, who later became first Chief of the Airborne Command and father of United States airborne doctrine. He adapted forest service techniques in organizing the first paratroop training base at Fort Benning, Georgia. Although the idea of aerial delivery of men was conceived as a military concept, it took the dedicated men of the forest service to prove it would work.

Each summer the smoke jumper schools are swamped by college students who learn firefighting and parachuting. The rugged training and conditioning received by the smoke jumper trainee is comparable to the military's program. A raging fire can be just as deadly as any enemy soldier, and more than one smoke jumper has lost his life to the flames. A branch of the Department of Agriculture, the Forest Service maintains several bases for the smoke jumper operations. However, the school and headquarters at Missoula, Montana, is the largest and best known. In contrast to the original handful of parachutists-turned-firefighters, in 1978 and 1979 a total of 795 smoke jumpers made 11,394 jumps to fight fires.

The Forest Service also has the edge on the Air Force's paramedic operations, having made its first rescue jumps back in 1940. That year smoke jumper

Tom Sutton is pictured hanging upside down from a trapeze as he descends during an exhibition parachute jump. In the old days a parachutist would occasionally get tangled in the lines and descend this way accidentally. (Ray Cottingham)

Chester N. Derry and Dr. Leo P. Martin parachuted into the Bitterroot Forest to aid victims of a plane crash. Although some pararescue work is still done by smoke jumpers, the Air Force teams usually handle this type of work now; their search-rescue operations are highly organized and their paramedics are specially trained.

These, then, are just some of the uses of the parachute and a brief account of the people who jump. Some jump to save their own lives—emergency—some jump to save the lives of others—testing and rescue. A few jump for money—exhibition—others jump for their country—military. But probably the greatest number jump for no other reason than just because it's fun. Parachuting for sport is difficult for the nonjumper to understand. All the other types of parachuting seem to have some practical reason behind them. But jumping into space thousands of feet above the ground just for the fun of it?

5. Soaring Without Wings

Free-Fall Parachuting

At one time there were only two types of parachuting: *free-fall* parachuting, in which the jumper activates the parachute by pulling a ripcord, and *static-line* jumping, in which the parachute is automatically opened by a line attached to the aircraft on one end and to the parachute on the other.

This is still basically true, and a jumper will normally log a jump as either a free-fall jump or a static-line jump. An example of free-fall jumping is the emergency jump when a pilot bails out and pulls the ripcord. An example of a static-line jump is the paratrooper who takes part in mass drops in military operations. Another example of static-line deployed parachutes is cargo dropping by parachute. Obviously a crate of ammunition cannot pull a ripcord, so the static line does the job.

More and more *automatic openers* are being used in all phases of parachute operations now, so this might be considered a third category. Most emergency jumps (actually nowadays these are usually ejections rather than jumps) are made with automatic openers. With these openers, which are operated either by a timer or by barometric pressure, the parachute is activated with a spring or explosive charge. There are a number of automatic openers available to the sport jumper, too. These are intended to operate as backup systems to activate the main or reserve parachute if the jumper fails to activate the parachute. Certainly the sport parachuting world owes a great deal to Steve Snyder for developing several automatic openers used extensively in sport parachuting. This writer can personally vouch for Snyder's reserve opener, having used it for several years. Snyder's files contain hundreds of letters from grateful persons who had their lives saved by his opener. For developing the reserve opener, Snyder was awarded the Leo Stevens medal, parachuting's highest award.

Free-fall parachuting itself can be divided into two categories: *controlled* free fall and *uncontrolled* free fall. A turn or backloop may indicate skill on the part of one jumper and be considered uncontrolled free fall on the part of another—the only difference being *intent*, not the maneuver itself. A beginning free-fall jumper will make many turns before learning to do one intentionally. The fact that you, as a student, made two right turns and a backloop is not very impressive if you're still hooked to your static line at the time.

In your early training jumps, with the chute deployed by a static line, you'll be concentrating on stability for the three or four seconds before the parachute opens. Your instructor will be watching to see that you learn to assume the basic stable spread position and hold it while the chute inflates, then later that you can remain stable while you reach in and pull the dummy ripcord. Finally, after half a dozen or so of these static-line jumps are done satisfactorily, the instructor will allow you to begin short free falls, at first no more than a "clear and pull," pulling the real ripcord just as you did the dummy ripcord. If you do these as instructed and maintain good control, your jumpmaster will begin moving you up to five-second delays and then ten-second delays. Then the real fun begins.

If it is any consolation to you as a student jumper, those first dozen jumps on the static line or on short free falls are actually more difficult than longer delays are. The reason is that you don't get the control of the air until about ten seconds after exit. Those first ten seconds are pretty much determined by your position when you leave the aircraft. It takes ten to twelve seconds for your body to accelerate to more than 100 mph, and like an airplane reaching flying speed, your body has now reached flying speed. Now you can control every movement by the position of your hands, feet, head, and entire body. But we're getting ahead of ourselves. . . .

Photographer-skydiver Carl Boenish gets "on the step" beside jump student Jean Campbell Boenish to film her first static-line jump. (Tom Sanders)

Under the watchful eyes of her jumpmaster (in the door), Jean steps back and arches her body while the static line pulls the pins to release her backpack. A Velcro fastener on the static line pulls the pilot chute out into the slipstream for a positive opening. (Carl Boenish)

"Arch-thousand" is the count as Jean holds a perfect stable arch and the sleeve-deployed canopy unfolds above her. (Carl Boenish)

"Look-thousand," as Jean holds her stable spread position and looks at the dummy rip-cord. The lines are now extended and the sleeve is being withdrawn from the canopy. (Carl Boenish)

"Pull-thousand" is the count as Jean reaches in to grip the dummy ripcord. As the canopy begins to inflate, she is pulled into the upright position. (Carl Boenish)

Opening shock bounces her like a puppet on a string as the canopy fully inflates and checks her fall. She is just starting to pull the dummy ripcord from its pocket. Free falling beside her, Carl filmed the jump in both motion pictures and stills. (Carl Boenish)

Professional photographer-skydiver Carl Boenish had his jumpsuit specially made for free-fall photography. He can float above a group for a high view, drop down under for a low-angle shot, and then "rise" back up above for still another view. (Bud Sellick)

Charts have been worked out that give you some idea of how far you will fall in a given length of time. In the earlier days of the sport, skydivers wore an instrument panel on their chest-mounted reserve parachute. This instrument board held two very important instruments: the altimeter and the stopwatch. According to the free-fall charts, the average body in a stable spread position would accelerate for the first twelve seconds and then fall at a constant speed. By the fifth second of free fall, the body has reached more than 70 mph. During the next six or seven seconds it will pick up another 40 to 50 mph, reaching a steady fall of between 110 and 120 mph, or 160–174 feet per second. By referring to your free-fall chart, you could have a pretty good idea of how far you would fall in a given length of time. If you planned to make a 30-second delay, for example, you would check the chart to see how far you would fall in 30 seconds (4,615 feet), added the opening altitude (2,500 feet), and knew you must make your jump from approximately 7,115 feet. But not necessarily. . . .

This is a good place to talk about free-fall charts. Ask a hundred people to tell you how to compute a chart of a falling body, and most won't even try. Two or three will, with a great deal of pride, announce that it's simple: a body falls at the rate of 32 feet per second, per second (32 fps^2). That's great for high school physics problems when you're dealing with a steel ball in a vacuum. But consider the variables the skydiver has to insert into his formula: size of jumper (long and lanky or short and stocky?), weight of jumper (skinny or fat?), type of jumpsuit (Sear's coveralls or Krueger Balloonsuit?), material of jumpsuit (cotton falls more slowly than nylon), type of parachute gear (conventional or piggy-back?), weight of parachutes (lightweight or conventional?), and even things like boots, helmet, and gloves. Think that does it? Nope. The position the jumper assumes is vital to the free-fall chart, too. Whether the jumper is flared out into a basic stable spread or tucked into a modified frog position makes a big difference. And diving or tracking across the sky also affects the rate of fall. Then you must figure temperature, humidity, and on and on. There are complicated aerodynamic drag force formulas available but we'll skip them.

So now you know that those free-fall charts are going to be very general rules of thumb used to give you some idea of how far you fall during a given length of time in a stable spread. USPA does not recognize any official rate-of-fall chart but requires "reasonable" times entered in your jump logbook. Matt McManus of the 1978 U.S. Parachute Team prepared a chart computed at 140 fps (95 mph), a more realistic rate with some of today's light parachute equipment and large, baggy jumpsuits. Most free-fall charts, prepared in the days of more conventional jumpsuits and parachutes, reflect 174 fps (120 mph). As a student or intermediate jumper, you are more likely to be wearing the traditional jumpsuits and parachutes, and the chart listed here is appropriate. By the time you have acquired the experience to jumpmaster yourself, you'll know how to read your altimeter and figure your delay in free fall.

Your ground training will cover the basics of your exit, stable spread position with strong back arch, emergency procedures, steering your parachute, and finally the parachute landing fall (PLF). Your qualified instructor will follow a prescribed training procedure that has been developed over several years by the best parachutists in the world and adopted by USPA.

In the appendix of this book is a list of USPA-affiliated sport parachute centers. To be affiliated centers, they must follow USPA basic safety regulations and doctrine for student and advanced skydivers. Affiliated centers also offer first-jump courses taught by USPA-certified instructors.

Once you have attained free-fall status and begun advancing into delayed drops, you can begin enjoying the sensations of free flight instead of worrying about holding the arch or making a good, solid exit. The position of the body as you begin your delay will determine the sensations you get. In the prone, face-to-earth position, there is little sensation of falling. But in the head high, standing position, you may experience the elevator effect momentarily, particularly if you look up at the plane as it appears to rush away from you.

Chart A / DISTANCE FALLEN IN FREE-FALL STABLE SPREAD POSITION

Seconds	Distance	Seconds	Distance	Seconds	Distance	Seconds	Distance
1	16	16	2179	31	4789	46	7399
2	62	17	2353	32	4963	47	7573
3	138	18	2527	33	5137	48	7747
4	242	19	2701	34	5311	49	7921
5	366	20	2875	35	5485	50	8095
6	504	21	3049	36	5659	51	8269
7	652	22	3223	37	5833	52	8443
8	808	23	3397	38	6007	53	8617
9	971	24	3571	39	6181	54	8791
10	1138	25	3745	40	6355	55	8965
11	1309	26	3919	41	6529	56	9139
12	1483	27	4093	42	6703	57	9313
13	1657	28	4267	43	6877	58	9487
14	1831	29	4441	44	7051	59	9661
15	2005	30	4615	45	7225	60	9835

Chart B / DISTANCE FALLEN EACH SECOND TO TERMINAL VELOCITY

Seconds	Distance
1	16
2	46
3	76
4	104
5	124
6	138
7	148
8	156
9	163
10	167
11	171
12	174

(Courtesy of Parachutes, Inc.)

As you drop away from the jump plane in a basic spread position, you become aware of the sudden silence that envelopes you—the sense of detachment that makes you feel more like an observer than a participant. You feel a strong wind blowing up from below and sense that you are accelerating even though the ground remains motionless, distant, and of no concern up here in this other world.

Remaining in the stable spread position, you feel your body slowing down as you approach terminal velocity of 174 fps, roughly 120 mph. From all outward sensations you have now ceased to fall, and you feel that you are floating in a strong wind . . . which is about what you are doing. Although still plummeting

48-way building (Carl Boenish)

Canopy opening shot of 50-way over Elsinore Drop Zone.
(Carl Boenish)

30-way building over Elsinore with Big Bear Mountain in background. (Carl Boenish)

Carl Boenish jumping specially made suit, Handbury Rig with 3 ring circus, Handbury reserve, and 35mm movie camera. (Ray Cottingham)

26-way star over Tahlequah, Oklahoma—world record at the time. Jump was organized by Jerry Bird and performed at 11th World Parachuting Championships. (Carl Boenish)

The "Flying Farkles" demonstrate basic star formation over Elsinore, California. (Carl Boenish)

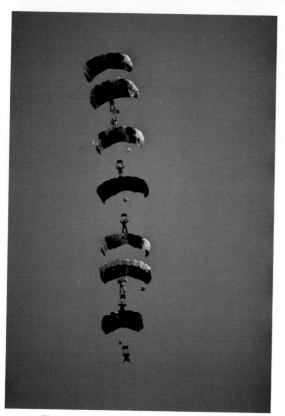

Skyvan Boogie, Canopy Relative Work. (© Bob Franks)

8-way double diamond over Casa Grande, Arizona, for movie *Wings*.

Cheryl Stearns' U.S. Flag jump into Liberty Island on July 4.
(Phil Rogge, USAPT)

Demonstration water jump at Chicago Air-Water Show. (Phil Rogge, USAPT)

Holding a perfect stable spread position, Jerry Rae displays the skydiver "fashion" for the 1980's. Boots are out and sneakers are in; colorful jumpsuits of moderate fullness; soft gloves and a soft leather French helmet; thin altimeter on the left wrist; lightweight full-view goggles; light (about 20 pounds total for both main and reserve) Handbury rig parachute system; and hand-deploy pilot chute. (Carl Boenish)

toward earth at 174 fps, you no longer feel the pull of gravity because it is equalized by the wind resistance against your body. You are balanced precariously on a huge column of air that has piled up beneath you, and the slightest off-balance movement will now throw you into a spin, backloop, barrel roll, or other unstable fall. Until you gain experience, you must concentrate on maintaining stability—no fancy aerobatics yet.

As you progress to longer delays, you will quickly learn that the stable spread position is more difficult to maintain after terminal velocity is reached than it is at the slower speeds. The rigid spread-eagle position used in the earlier static-line training jumps will now result in constant buffeting, pitching, and yawing. Now is the time to relax into the frog position with the legs and arms bent and the hands comfortably near the shoulders. In the frog position the rate of descent is greater than in the basic spread position. Control is more precarious now because the body is drawn up into a smaller area. In the event you suddenly find yourself inverted (it's likely on the early attempts) and looking up at the sky instead of down at the ground, simply arch your back and spread your arms and legs back to the basic stable spread. Within a second or two you will be back in the face-to-earth position and stable . . . and can try again.

The basic spread-eagle position with the arched back is the answer to any uncontrolled fall and will result in instant recovery to the face-to-earth position. The only possible exception is the flat spin, which is difficult to stop but easy to avoid. When you feel yourself turning to one side or the other, you must immediately twist your body to counter it. The hands, feet, trunk, and head can all be employed either to initiate a turn or to stop it. If a spin becomes fast and you cannot otherwise counter it, sweep your arms back to the sides and bend forward at the waist. This will cause a forward tumble and break the flow of air that is supporting the spin. After a tumble or two, arch your back and throw your arms and legs out in the basic spread position. Almost instantly you will be stable in a face-to-earth position. It is best to avoid letting any turns develop into spins.

Once you have learned to maintain stability and to recover from uncontrolled free fall, you can begin concentrating on free-fall maneuvers. After some experience, you will find yourself making turns, loops, and rolls without any conscious effort at all. Although employing various techniques, you will be able to do them as effortlessly as when turning around on the ground—actually more easily. To explain in words how to maintain stability and how to execute turns is something like trying to explain how to balance and steer a bicycle to someone who has never even been on a bicycle. There are certain basics to know, but from then on, it's a matter of doing it until it becomes second nature.

There are two main points to keep in mind when learning aerobatics: (1) establish a reference point on the ground and use it to maintain a firm heading, and (2) start from a flat, stable position with the horizon comfortably visible to the front. With these two references determined before beginning, you can accomplish precision turns, loops, and rolls, and always end the maneuver exactly where it began. It is imperative to keep your eyes open and not lose sight of reference points more than is necessary. Obviously, if you don't know where you are when starting a maneuver, there is no way of knowing when you have finished it, either.

TURNS

Basically there are three types of turns: *hand* turns, *foot* turns, and *body* turns. However, accomplished jumpers employ combinations of these and come up with some unique ideas of their own.

It was once thought there were *only* these three basic turns. Later modifications of these turns included the arms and legs. Then the hand turn was supplemented by the push turn, which combined with the arms and body until virtually every part of the body is now employed in making such fast turns that judging is nearly impossible. To the untrained eye, some of the champion-style (free-fall maneuvering) jumpers appear to be tumbling and spinning in totally uncontrolled fall. In reality, they are making precision 360-degree turns to the right and left with backloops . . . in roughly seven seconds! By drawing the body up into a tight button-like position they can execute turns with lightning speed.

The story persists that Loy Brydon, on a competition-style jump, removed his helmet in free fall and simply swung it from his head to his rear and back a couple of times. In the tight position it appeared to the judges on the ground that he had completed his series of turns and loops in record-breaking time. Brydon neither denied nor confirmed the story. However anybody who has tried to judge a style event, even using modern optics, finds the story quite feasible.

Hand turns are always done from the relaxed frog position, where the body offers a minimum of resistance and can easily spin about its axis or center of gravity. To execute a hand turn to the right, for example, you tilt the hands at a 45-degree angle so the heel of the right hand is down and the heel of the left hand is up. To increase the force, you may push the right hand down while the left hand remains in the shoulder-high position. To stop the turn and reverse directions, roll the hands over to the other side so the left hand is low with the heel down and the heel of the right hand is now up. This is essentially the same principle as a propeller's twist.

Foot turns and leg turns are accomplished by raising and lowering the feet and legs. The body will swing toward the lower foot and away from the higher foot. To turn to the left, for example, the legs must swing to the right, so the right leg and foot are simply lowered while the left leg and foot are left high. The positions are reversed to stop the turn and initiate a turn in the opposite direction.

Body turns are nearly always combined with arms and hands. The body is simply twisted to the right or left so the shoulder toward the turn is slightly lower than the other—again this is like the twist of a propeller.

THE BACKLOOP

The backloop is one of the simplest aerial maneuvers to accomplish: no matter how sloppy the attempt, a loop (actually a backward somersault or back-flip) is nearly sure to result. However, a clean execution of any maneuver is necessary in style competition both from the standpoint of proper performance in the eyes of the judges and in terms of the time element. Lost seconds are lost points in competition, and flailing around in the sky in an attempt to "swim" through a given maneuver takes too much time. No judge will award the full number of points for sloppy maneuvers no matter how fast they are performed, so the loop must be both fast and clean.

To accomplish a loop or any other maneuver properly, you must establish yourself in relation to the ground and the horizon. First, select a reference point on the ground (a runway, highway, or fencerow). Second, make sure that you are starting from a flat stable position with the horizon comfortably visible in

Bob Johns demonstrates a backloop for the camera. (Carl Boenish)

front, rather than too high or too low. With these two references determined before the start of a maneuver, precision turns, loops, and rolls can be accomplished with the maneuver always ending exactly where it began.

There is a tendency to roll off on one side during the backloop, but an understanding of the aerodynamics involved can correct the problem. Keeping the arms and legs spread gives a maximum of control over the rolling. However, putting the arms or legs close together is sometimes necessary to accomplish a clean maneuver. Each person must therefore adjust according to his or her need, spreading sometimes to gain stability and control, closing at other times to gain speed. In the illustrations you will seldom see a true textbook example of how any given maneuver is accomplished, because each individual alters the basic positions to suit personal needs. It is sometimes necessary to alter a position and even completely violate a standard or accepted method in order to achieve the speed and attitude desired.

A backloop starts from the basic face-to-earth position. The arms are extended out and forward as the knees are drawn up to the body. This will swing the body up into an upright, seated position. The arms sweep down past the hips as if jumping rope, causing the body to fall over backward. The initial action of extending the arms and drawing up the knees will be enough to carry the body over the top of the loop into the inverted position. As the horizon comes back into view, the legs are extended and the arms moved back to the original stable spread position to prevent a continuation of the loop beyond the original horizontal position. As the initial reference point on the ground comes back into view, the flared-out, basic spread position is assumed.

Disorientation during early attempts is common. As a novice you may finish the loop as much as 90 degrees off the original heading. You might also find yourself tilted over on one side, with the horizon apparently standing vertical in front of you.

FRONTLOOP

The frontloop is usually done by accident a few times before the novice learns to maintain a stable position. Improper arch and looking down at the ground on exit during initial static-line student jumps often result in a forward loop. Later, as you begin free falls, you may execute a frontloop while pulling the ripcord, particularly with the two-hand method while looking at the ripcord. Again, it results from looking down and losing the arch. With this thought in mind, the skilled jumper can easily accomplish frontloops with precision. Starting from a stable spread or relaxed frog position, tuck the chin down, roll the shoulders forward, and extend the legs. Sweep the arms back to a delta position or even bring them in to the sides as the body is bent sharply at the waist. The body immediately noses over and the legs are swung upward in a shuttlecock effect. This initiates a forward tumble or loop. Bending the legs and extending the arms slightly as the horizon appears again (upside down) will keep the body rotating while the hands and arms help prevent roll. As the body reaches the upright position and the horizon appears rightside up dead ahead, swing the arms forward into a high spread to stop the rotation. The body then flares out into a stable spread position.

BARREL ROLL

Like the backloop, the barrel roll is a simple maneuver—except faster, like a snaproll in an airplane. The reference point on the horizon is the secret. Keep your eyes glued to that reference point on the horizon the entire time so the body remains prone whether face-to-earth or back-to-earth or in between. A barrel roll is a fast maneuver that is little more than a swish of the right arm and a swish of the left. It is started from the basic spread position with the legs fully extended and only slightly separated. For a clockwise roll, the left arm remains extended, but the right arm is pulled in to the chest. The body will instantly roll

Students and experts alike know the first thing to do after pulling the rip-cord is to "check your canopy" and see if it's properly inflated. Don't panic if it looks like this tangled mess at first. It will almost always clear itself immediately. Reaching up and separating the risers will speed the process. Sometimes a minor malfunction can be shaken loose. If things don't clear up then, it's time to cut away from the mess and open your reserve. (Carl Boenish)

Determining what is exactly straight down can be very difficult from high altitudes. Everything within a one-mile radius looks like it's directly below. The ability to "spot" yourself and others and exit at the right point in space was critical in the days before the high-performance parachutes were developed. (Carl Boenish)

One of the jumpers on this mass drop got a little careless going through the door and didn't protect the ripcord on the reserve. Serious injury is possible from being struck by the tail of the aircraft. Not only is being left at 12,000 feet hanging under an inflated canopy embarrassing, but the long ride down gets pretty uncomfortable.
(Ray Cottingham)

Willie Manbo and Ed McKay collided while attempting to get into a star, dislodging Willie's reserve at about 5,000 feet. Willie was involved in a canopy collision earlier. (See photos pp. 137) (Carl Boenish)

over in the back-to-earth position and momentum is maintained by extending the right arm as the left is withdrawn to the chest. The roll will continue back to the face-to-earth position and the left arm is quickly reextended to prevent overshooting. Each arm is withdrawn for no more than a second before being reextended.

BACK-TO-EARTH POSITION

The back-to-earth position is the most relaxed position a free-fall jumper can assume, but it requires concentrated effort to avoid turns and uncontrolled spinning. A jumper who loses consciousness in free fall will always roll onto his or her back and begin turning. To roll onto the back, extend one arm and withdraw the other for a second—then reextend immediately. Loss of arch nearly always results in an inverted position. Students on early static-line jumps learn this very quickly. To get back in the face-to-earth position, arch the body and get the head back. Jumpers should make a conscious effort to experiment with back-to-earth delays periodically: they are unique, unpredictable, and exhilarating.

A side note here is appropriate. The style event (free-fall maneuvers) in competition has begun to fall from popularity in favor of the more satisfying relative work (flying in relation to others) "sequential" events. One of the reasons is that the style event is approaching the limit of human ability. Dozens of style contestants will perform the same international series of turns and loops within just a few hundredths of a second of each other, and the skill becomes more one of judging than of competing. To put some added difficulty back into the event, it might be done from the inverted position in future competitions. The same could be true of relative work. Can you imagine the difficulty of performing four-way and eight-way events in the back-to-earth position? Or of alternating contestants in sequential events so that half of the contestants are in the face-to-earth position while the other half are in the back-to-earth position? Many relative work maneuvers are complicated by having some people "back in" rather than fly straight in, so having a few inverted should add another element of fun. If the thought of mixing back-to-earth maneuvers into style and relative work events seems ridiculous, don't forget, so did the thought of doing canopy relative work just a few years ago. Skydivers are very creative people. If there is a way to make a simple maneuver just a little more challenging, they will think of it. If a challenging maneuver can be made impossible, everybody will try it. And before you know it, somebody will succeed and the race will be on for the next challenge.

The ability to initiate a given maneuver and then return to a stable fall is basic and essential to safety and enjoyment in the sport of parachuting. While there are some basic, elementary maneuvers that are sure to be a part of any competition, there is no limit to the combination of maneuvers you can accomplish if you thoroughly understand the aerodynamic forces that act upon your body. If you remember that you are balanced on a huge ball of air, you can understand why certain things happen when you move your body in certain ways. With this basic knowledge, you can invert maneuvers and experiment with positions to see what happens. These can be planned on the ground and then tried in the air. But remember that like an airplane, the human body requires ample altitude for experimentation to allow enough time to recover stability above the minimum opening altitude.

Those of us who began experimenting with maneuvers in free fall before established positions were discovered had great fun plunging out and assuming certain positions just to see what happened. Completely uncontrolled fall is exciting when recovery to stable fall is always within immediate reach, but uncontrolled fall is sheer terror when recovery is not within the jumper's grasp. Clawing a ripcord from its pocket while in chaotic tumbles and spins, I've seen that glob of unsheathed canopy shoot past my legs, trailed by a writhing mass of tangled lines. In those split-second lifetimes I've heard myself screaming warnings from some detached point in time and space, and when, somehow, all the lines clear themselves and the canopy blasts open, the shock jolts me back to reality. I am no longer viewing experience from some remote vantage point, but am a flesh-and-blood participant. Often a tiny trickle of blood verifies this truth, where a buckle digs into a shoulder or a connector link grazes the ear.

David Blattel hand-deploys his pilot chute high over Elsinore Drop Zone. Hand deploys have replaced ripcords in many rigs, offering a more positive opening. Fellow skydiver Carl Boenish caught this scene with a rear-facing camera mounted on his helmet. (Carl Boenish)

Early experiments with uncontrolled free fall and the recovery to stability were done without the benefit of padded harnesses or deployment devices. This meant that the position assumed at the time the ripcord was pulled was likely to be the position held at the moment of opening shock. All of us had heard the gory stories of those head-down openings in which the victims dived out of their harnesses. Yet, there are few old-timers who have had their helmets ripped from their head in a head-down opening—frequently giving up a small portion of skin with the helmet.

Today, with modern sport equipment, experimentation can still be as thrilling without being quite so punishing. The final test of skill for the jumper who thinks he or she can contend with any situation is that one hilarious fling into space without any attempt to stabilize. Somersault, spin, and flip-flop around the sky for a few thousand feet until the only reference point is your own body and your instruments (*never* lose track of time or altitude!), then flare out into a stable spread and enjoy the feeling of power that comes with gaining perfect control from total chaos. This stage is reached only after thorough mastery of body control and the ability to quickly and accurately read your altimeter during total disorientation.

INSTRUMENTS

After acquiring a degree of confidence in yourself and your equipment, having made a dozen or more jumps, you can begin using instruments. This used to consist of a stopwatch and an altimeter, although most of today's jumpers use only the altimeter.

The altimeter may be one especially designed and manufactured for the sport or it may be a standard (sensitive) aircraft altimeter. The sport type are lighter, easier to read, and more compact. Because of the rough treatment during routine parachuting operations, a jumper should make a habit of checking the accuracy of his or her altimeter often, and should never make the mistake of relying solely on instruments during long delays. The altimeter can be checked against the aircraft altimeter during the ascent to jump altitude and should be checked again at the time of exit to be sure the instrument is reading approximately the same as the aircraft. Both should be set at zero on the ground so the reading is the true altitude above the field and not elevation above sea level. In large jump planes with several skydivers you can check your altimeter against those of jumpers near you. Also, if the jump craft is being flown in controlled airspace, your pilot may prefer to keep the aircraft altimeter calibrated to sea level for communications with air traffic control and other planes in the area.

During the actual free fall, you must not keep your eyes glued to the altimeter, but read it periodically while also scanning the horizon (to maintain

The instrument that is a must for every skydiver is the altimeter. The popular one is the Altimaster that came on the market in the early 1960's. (SSE, Inc.)

stable orientation), the ground below, and the sky (for fellow jumpers). Your altimeter can be wrong, so never rely entirely on it. Also look at the drop zone below, the target area, and other references. If you discover that everyone else is pulling, chances are that you should be too.

The audible altimeter, *Paralert*, was developed by Steve Snyder especially for relative workers. It eliminates the need to look away from fellow jumpers to read the dial on the altimeter. The Paralert altitude warning device beeps at any preselected altitude between 2,500 and 4,500 feet above the ground. When you reach your selected altitude, the Paralert emits a pulsating tone. It is light and compact enough to be easily mounted on the helmet or soft hat, and uses the same solid-state circuitry as SSE Incorporated's MK2000 automatic opener.

Obviously a thorough knowledge of the table of free-fall rate of descent is necessary before you engage in free-fall delayed jumps. Prior to takeoff, you should decide how many seconds' delay you plan to make. For example, if you are going to make a 30-second delay, you know from the free-fall table that you will fall approximately 4,600 feet. In order to open at a safe 2,500 feet above the ground, you must jump from at least 7,100 feet. As you drop away from the jump plane and begin your free fall, you can actually see the altimeter winding down (at roughly 174 feet per second, if you hold a stable spread position). Most of the time you'll be jumping with other jumpers around you. Your fellow jumpers should be giving a wave-off signal about the same time you are. Meanwhile, keep looking around you and below you, and don't trust your life to any mechanical warning system. If in doubt, give a wave-off to the others and pull. Don't wait

Free-Fall Parachuting 131

The audible altimeter buckled to the helmet, Paralert, beeps to let the skydiver know when the preselected altitude is reached. It is especially helpful during relative work when you don't want to take your eyes off those around you. (SSE, Inc.)

for the other person to pull or you may both be in for a surprise. I had just such a surprise while I was taking free-fall pictures of fellow skydiver Jack Norman, Jr., of Nashville. Because I was busy with the camera rather than watching my altimeter or the ground, I decided to pull when I saw Jack pull. Unfortunately, we had not discussed this prior to the jump. Jack was busy posing for pictures and planning to pull when I did. As we were passing through 1,000 feet, my automatic opener released my reserve and I came to a jarring halt. Jack saw my reserve opening and pulled his main. We both landed safely and much smarter. The best safety device in the sport of parachuting is one that has evolved over many years—your brain. Use it.

RATE OF DESCENT

Remember there is more to free-falling than just falling. The uninformed may observe of sport parachutists that any nut can fling himself or herself from a plane and drop like a rock. This premise is not totally inaccurate, although even dropping straight down requires stability, and stability requires locking into a basic stable spread position for most jumpers (exceptions later). As discussed earlier, this position is assumed by extending the arms out from the shoulders with the legs extended and slightly spread. Knees and elbows can be comfortably bent and you can relax, provided there is always a balance of aerodynamic forces. If you are out of balance on top of that column of air, you'll be the first to know about it. Again, think of yourself as being balanced on a huge ball of air that "rolls" with you. If you lean forward, you'll tumble forward. Tilt to the left or right and you'll slide off in that direction. Shift your center of gravity to the back and you'll backslide.

Many jumpers have encountered difficulty at some time with their goggles

If you're in a hurry to get down, this dive position will do the trick by increasing your free-fall speed from the 120 mph range to the 200 mph range. Even the toes are pointed to lessen drag. This is a still of Dave Wilds from the short feature *Sky Dive*. (Carl Boenish)

Gary Patmore, in a relaxed frog position, flies patrol among the billowing clouds. (Carl Boenish)

during a free-fall jump. If the hands are pulled up to the face to secure the goggles back in place, the result will be an immediate nose dive. The front half of the body has nothing to support it, while the back half has legs extending. The skydiver becomes a human shuttlecock. This "Y" position results in a higher rate of descent; the jumper may continue to accelerate to speeds of 160 to 200 mph instead of the so-called "terminal velocity" of the spread position, which is about 120 mph. A man named Canarrozzo popularized this position by folding the arms across the chest. Some skydivers also cross their arms behind their back to achieve this same diving position when speed is desired. However, it is possible to reach up with both hands and adjust your goggles without going into a Canarrozzo nose dive. Bend the legs back at the knees to reduce drag at the rear while extending the elbows to increase drag up front. The resultant balance of forces allows you to assume a relatively stable position. Many of the large jumpsuits used by relative workers and free-fall photographers have cloth extensions between the waist and elbow that help increase or decrease drag as the elbows are extended or withdrawn. When the body is drawn up into a tighter position, the frog position described earlier, the area of drag is reduced and the rate of fall will increase slightly. This position allows the free-falling jumper to remain prone and horizontal to the surface, yet fall faster than in the full spread position.

The rate of fall can be adjusted by adjusting the amount of area the body covers.

Rate of fall can also be adjusted by the type of clothing worn. Large, baggy jumpsuits slow the jumper's descent, while tight-fitting jumpsuits increase speed. A large person falls faster than a small person, if both wear identical clothing and assume identical positions. Therefore, if a large and a small person are performing free-fall maneuvers in relation to each other, they will have to adjust positions to maintain identical rates of descent. The smaller, lighter person will have to draw up into a tighter position to fall slightly faster, while the larger person will flare out into a larger spread to fall more slowly. In addition, if the larger person wore a loose-fitting jumpsuit while the smaller person wore a tight-fitting jumpsuit, their difference in rate of fall would be considerably less than if they both wore identical clothing.

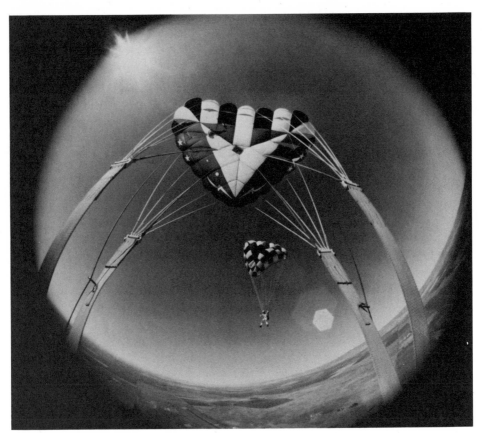

Security Thunderbows over Yolo, California, as seen through fish-eye lens. These delta-shaped canopies reached the market in the early Seventies but were no match for the "squares." (Ray Cottingham)

TRACKING

Departing from the stable spread or frog positions which allow the jumper to maintain a flat, horizontal position will result in a gliding effect. These positions allow the jumper to glide, or track, as much as a one-to-one ratio. The variations of *the delta position* determine the efficiency of the track. In the delta position, the legs remain extended and slightly spread, while the arms are swept back in varying degrees from the shoulder level. The hands always remain flat, fingers together (gloves help considerably), to act as ailerons and give control on the latitudinal axis. There is a tendency to roll as the arms are drawn down closer to the body, and the rudder-like effect of the hands prevents this. A *medium delta position* is maintained by extending the arms at about 45 degrees from the shoulder toward the waist. In this position, the body tends to tilt forward and slide or glide downhill. The rate of descent increases because the air is being deflected to the rear rather than being piled up beneath the body as in the stable fall. There is no aerodynamic lift created by this downhill glide, however, and this increased rate of forward speed is quickly neutralized by the increased rate of descent. Obviously, the longer time the body can glide, the farther it can go, but this time is reduced by the rapid descent. There is an optimum glide ratio that each skydiver must determine for himself or herself, and this optimum glide cannot be appreciably increased.

It has been determined that a jumper may attain a horizontal speed of roughly 60 mph in the delta position. The danger involved in two jumpers approaching each other from opposite directions at up to 60 mph is obvious. Yet this is frequently the case when two inexperienced free-fallers attempt relative work, such as a hook-up, before they fully understand the forces involved. Unfortunately, midair collisions account for a significant number of injuries and fatalities in the sport. More experienced free-falling jumpers learn to approach at reduced speeds and then in such a way as to pass just to one side rather than head-on. Steve Snyder's automatic opener has saved a number of lives when the victim of "freight-training" regains consciousness under an inflated reserve chute. But too many have been knocked unconscious who did not have an automatic opener. Automatic openers that deploy the main parachute are also available for sport jumping.

For maximum tracking the delta position is modified into the *"max-track" position*. In the maximum-track position, the body is humped in such a way that the larger, thicker portion of the head and shoulders creates an airfoil and actually gives a certain amount of lift. The head is drawn back and the shoulders are rolled forward, legs remain extended and arms are bent slightly and drawn in near the sides. Hands are cupped slightly and held near the hips. The body should be maintained in a head-down attitude at about 30 degrees below the

A major cause of parachuting fatalities is the midair collision of jumpers or of jumpers with canopies. When striking a canopy, the upper jumper usually suffers severe lacerations while the lower jumper is knocked unconscious after having his canopy destroyed. Carl Boenish was filming Ken Vos (left) and Willie Manbo (right) at close range and then began drifting back for a long-range view as Vic Weatherford opened below. (The lower jumper always has the "right of way.") Boenish just missed hitting the canopy himself as his camera recorded this jumper's nightmare. Vos and Manbo snapped 13 suspension lines, each line having a tensile strength of 550 pounds. Vos was hospitalized for several days with a broken jaw, cracked ribs, and severe facial lacerations that required plastic surgery. Manbo was hospitalized with a fractured shoulder. Weatherford's canopy was destroyed, but he landed safely on his reserve chute. All three recovered to jump again. (Carl Boenish)

Gary Patmore and Roger Railey rendezvous in the solitude of inner space. Although forward speeds may approach 60 mph, they approach each other gently. (Carl Boenish)

horizontal. This position will vary from one individual to another; each must determine his or her own optimum max-track position through experimentation. The rate of descent is greater than in a basic spread position and even as great as in a medium delta. The difference is in the significantly greater horizontal movement.

The ability to track, or move horizontally, during the descent before the chute is opened is helpful in correcting errors in spotting. When several persons are exiting the aircraft on the same pass over the target area, the person who spots and determines the exit point may make an error. Even assuming he is correct, the first person to leave and the last person to leave are separated horizontally by the speed of the aircraft during that span of time. Obviously both jumpers cannot be exactly in the right place in space. The first jumper may hold a stable spread position, while the last person has to turn around and track back several hundred yards to get back to the proper point where he or she can reach the target after opening.

The ability to track can also prevent some embarrassing situations. A former jump student of mine and I were making a fun jump for accuracy only, but from 7,500 feet with a 30-second delay. We had been jumping at different clubs and had not jumped together for more than a year. During this time, he had purchased the recently developed Para-Commander chute and was becoming fairly accurate. I was wearing my favorite old rag—a 7-TU modification with nearly 300 jumps on it. He insisted that I spot for us, since I had such an old chute and could not maneuver as well as he. He said that I should spot for myself to be in the best possible place and that he would exit immediately behind me. Even though he might be a little farther out than I, he could easily bomb the target in his P-C, he explained. I smiled and thanked him for his kindness to old has-beens like myself and agreed to do the spotting. As we made our final jump run toward the target, I got out early and signaled the student to get ready. He crowded up to the door as I positioned on the wheel outside. I nodded for him to follow and pushed away nearly a mile short of the target—then humped into a max-track and hoped he wasn't watching me. He wasn't. I landed respectably in the target area and had finished a Coke back at the hangar when he arrived on horseback from an adjoining farm.

More than one visitor has been initiated into a new club by having the group take him or her far off the spot and then all track back to the right point, leaving the visitor a mile or two off in the wrong direction.

To correct a bad spot—whether it was intentional or not—is not too diffi-

Until the Seventies, about the only way you could be part of a mass drop of 40 or more parachutists was to join the Army and storm out the door on a dope-rope. Many sport parachute centers have DC-3's for full-time use. Here Dave Wilds leads a team of skydivers out in a scene from the movie *Sky Dive*. (Carl Boenish)

cult. When jumping with jokesters or others whom you suspect might be leading you astray, it is a good idea to keep an eye on them as you follow them out of the plane. If you see the other jumpers humping their shoulders and assuming a max-track, it's a good idea to swing around and follow them. If you find you cannot reach the proper opening point even by tracking, you may have an alternate method of reaching the target. If you are upwind of the target, simply open high (but be sure the sky above you is clear if others are jumping with you). By opening high, you remain in the air longer and drift with the wind longer. The farther out you are, the higher you must open if you are to remain aloft long enough to reach the target area. Conversely, if you find you are downwind of the target or nearly over it, a low opening (but no lower than safety rules permit) will allow you to reach the ground sooner and prevent drifting farther than is absolutely necessary.

JUMPING WITH OTHERS

When jumping alone or with only one or two others whom you can keep in constant view during free fall, a high opening creates no hazard. However, when a group of jumpers is falling together, under no circumstances should the canopy be deployed above the jointly agreed-upon opening altitude. Even when the agreed opening point is reached, it is a good idea for the parachutist to give the wave-off signal to any possible jumpers directly over him. The wave-off is given by sweeping the hands from the outstretched basic spread position in toward the head and back, bending the arms at the elbows.

Smart jumpers avoid being near other jumpers below 4,000 feet. If they find themselves immediately over another jumper at 3,000 feet, they should make every effort to get away while being especially alert for the jumper below to pull. If this occurs, the pilot chute can be batted aside. In the days of unsleeved canopies, it would be almost impossible to avoid entanglement. However, because of the sleeve-deployment or bag-deployment, the opening is slowed, and the upper jumper can escape by keeping alert. An alternate choice when directly over another jumper as the opening altitude is approached is to give a wave-off signal and pull slightly higher. These are situations that will not occur among skilled free-fall jumpers, who avoid ever getting into such a predicament. When planning the jump, before boarding the aircraft, all jumpers should agree on the opening altitude.

RELATIVE WORK

After you are proficient in the aerial maneuvers (when you can adjust your rate of descent in free fall and can move horizontally) you are sure to engage in relative work (RW), that is, jumping in relation to other skydivers. In the early days,

Careful planning on the ground is important when jumping with others. Here the skydivers are "dirt diving" before getting airborne. (Bud Sellick)

RW was limited to only a few jumpers taking pictures of each other or passing an object. As the sport grew, so did the size of the jump planes being used. That meant that more people could get into the air at one time. Instead of using a four-place Cessna, large DC-3's became the thing and forming large "stars" or lattice-work formations became commonplace. Most experienced skydivers agree that this is the real fun of the sport. That sense of weightlessness is most apparent during relative work. To see other human beings drifting serenely around you, gently rising and settling as they approach, is an experience second to none.

Before becoming involved in those large formations, you will first practice RW with only one or two other skydivers. You should practice everything on the ground beforehand, of course. This is called "dirt diving." Whether there are only two or a hundred, everybody must know exactly what he or she will be doing from the time the aircraft is entered until the aircraft is exited, as well as what is to be done during the actual free-fall portion of the RW jump.

At this early stage of the game you'll want to begin RW with somebody who is already proficient; it may be your jumpmaster or other qualified person you trust. After the two of you have decided that this first attempt will be a simple "hookup" (joining hands and falling together for several seconds), you walk it through on the ground, including the exit from the plane. Normally, the novice

Sonny Yates had about 300 jumps to his credit when he lost his eyesight. Wearing a tiny radio (white box on helmet) to receive instructions for opening and steering to the target, he made more than 20 jumps while totally blind. (Carl Boenish)

RW jumper will exit first and try to maintain a stable free-fall position while the more experienced RW jumper will do the flying and will pin the first person. Walk each step through, exiting the aircraft on the ground as your partner follows you; holding your position as your partner circles back and closes in; and finally making contact—in this case, probably simply joining hands. With larger groups, the "grip" may be on your sleeve or the leg of your jumpsuit. But for this first two-way hookup, you'll join hands. Once everything is predetermined, including the break-off signal and opening altitude, you're ready to go.

At jump altitude, you dive out and flare out into a basic stable spread position as your partner dives out after you. As your free-fall rate of descent accelerates to more than 100 mph, you'll begin to buffet, pitch, and yaw in the basic spread position. Bending your arms and knees, you relax into the more comfortable, yet very stable, frog position. Now, with only slight movements of your hands or feet, you can pivot your body to keep your partner in view as he or she approaches your level. You are surprised at how effortlessly and naturally you are turning. Your job at this point is to stay in one spot and fall straight down, like going down an elevator shaft without hitting the sides. Most of the time you'll be drifting off the vertical and actually sliding off slightly in one direction or another. This makes it more difficult for your partner to intercept your path of flight but he or she will make it look easy. As your partner closes slowly to within a few feet, you reach out to join hands. To your surprise, your partner drifts backward away from you. You find yourselves separated by several feet again. You wonder why your partner backed away from you as you resume the relaxed frog position once more. Actually what has happened was that *you* backed away from your partner. When you slowly extended your hands to your partner while your legs remained in the slightly tucked position, the front portion of your body rose higher than the rear portion, causing you to slide backward. Lesson number one: *don't reach*. You can see your instructor's legs straighten slightly as he or she drifts smoothly toward you again. Now you know why your partner didn't reach out before to take your hands. Like a spacecraft docking in orbit, the two of you join hands just before your smiling faces touch. Now securely joined together, physically and emotionally, the two of you slowly revolve around each other as a unit. Alternately bending or extending your legs makes you turn one way, then stop, then turn the other. At 3,500 feet your partner will relax the grip and slowly push away from you. You both turn 180 degrees and track in opposite directions for maximum separation on opening altitude of 2,500 feet.

Notice that these RW body maneuvers are always done slowly or slightly.

Handicaps won't keep good people down, even in skydiving. Here Chuck Anderson and Al (Captain Hook) Krueger, literally, "hook up." One of the most-liked men in the sport, Al has won both national and world champion titles. (Carl Boenish)

When you extended your arms slowly toward your partner, you simply slid backward, but if you had extended your arms abruptly, you would have done a backloop. Extending the legs slowly pushed you forward, but extending them abruptly would have resulted in a forward somersault. So now you're learning that the same movements can give different results, depending on the abruptness of that movement.

After gaining some confidence—and a great deal of enthusiasm—in a few successful hookups, you will progress to the next level of RW training, called no-contact relative work. Again, you go first and your instructor dives out after you. By now you're able to exit and quickly assume a stable frog position without losing control. Your instructor closes to within five or six feet in front of you and then holds that position. Now it becomes a game of follow-the-leader. Your instructor will drop a few feet lower and you must drop down to that level; then your partner will rise up a few feet above you and you must rise up to that level, too. This accomplished successfully, your partner moves back to the left and you move back to the left. This is harder than you thought after those "easy" hookups made earlier. You discover it's one thing to get close enough to grab hands and hang on, but a totally different thing to get close and stay close without the benefit of a good grip. You don't understand (or appreciate) the difficulty of your instructor's task to remain stationary while you struggle to get back into position. In the "old" days before RW techniques had been discovered, two skydivers would chase each other around the sky for thousands of feet in an unsuccessful attempt to get close enough to pass a baton. Finally somebody came up with the bright idea of one person staying in one spot while the other person did the maneuvering. That was quite a revelation at the time. And it holds true today, even with those huge megaformations. Somewhere in that enormous lattice-work is one base person who is the nucleus around which the entire formation is assembled. More about that later, though.

The third phase of your RW training starts the same as phase two. You exit, then your instructor exits behind you and approaches you at your level. But this time your instructor will stop about 30 feet away from you. Now the instructor becomes the stationary person and you must go to him or her. You'll learn that moving forward too quickly will cause you to dive below and past your partner. After you've turned around and set yourself up again, you approach again, this time much slower. Your proficiency is improving with each attempt. Soon flying becomes as natural as walking. You find yourself making subtle movements of the body and arms and legs without consciously thinking about them. If you approach too fast, your instructor will sideslip to the right and let you thunder past like a charging bull after the matador. By now you're not only doing things instinctively, but you're learning the flight characteristics of your partner

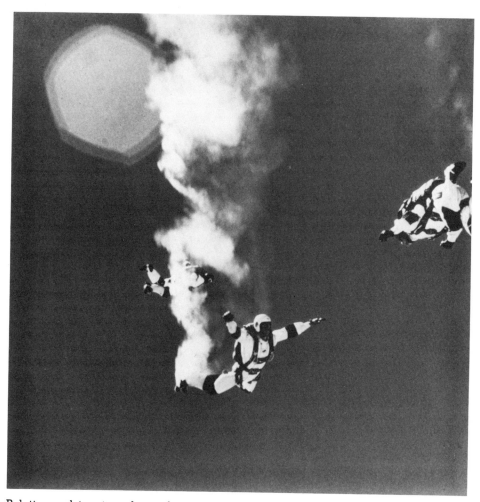

Relative work is extremely satisfying when it's done right. Here one skydiver holds the base position while the others move in. (Carl Boenish)

as well. You've developed that sixth sense that tells you to zig when your partner zigs and to zag when your partner zags.

The final phase of your formal RW training is reversing roles with your instructor. The instructor goes first and waits for you to do the flying and make the contact. At this point you're combining all the skills learned in the previous phases and you'll be surprised at how easily you followed your partner out and quickly moved right into position for a smooth contact. You've learned the skills that enable you to take part in larger RW jumps without endangering yourself or others.

Trying to complete a formation with other jumpers, you may be tempted beyond established safety margins to make one last effort. It could very likely be just that. (Carl Boenish)

An ample amount of time is required for early RW attempts and, in sport parachuting, time is altitude. Never become so involved in relative work that awareness of altitude and time is lost. If the contact is not made by 4,000 feet, the wave-off should be given and the jumpers should get clear of each other for the remaining 1,500 to 2,000 feet before opening. This is a good safety margin and it should not be shortened even though there is an almost irrepressible urge to continue when contact is only inches away. Sometimes those last few inches can take too long. A second attempt may never be possible, if this one is pursued beyond the realm of safety. In 1974 three skydivers from Windhoek, S.W. Africa, finally got their three-way together at about 150 feet off the ground. All three pulled their ripcords but died instantly on impact before the parachutes had cleared the containers.

By the time you are ready for RW jumps on a mass scale, you will no longer be trying to conquer basic skills but will be looking for new challenges. With large groups the dirt diving becomes even more essential, of course. With groups of six or more skydivers, the recommended break-off altitude is 4,000 feet. The separation and opening become especially crucial with large groups of skydivers. Immediately upon releasing grips, the RW jumpers should turn 180 degrees and track away from the center of the formation to get maximum separation for the wave-off and pull, just as with small groups. From the spectators' view below, this separation looks like a spectacular bomb-burst. In very large formations, the openings are sometimes staggered. The base person initiates it by releasing the pilot chute at 4,000 feet. They all release their grip, turn, and track away. Like a huge wedding cake, the ring of skydivers closest to the center will open at 3,500 feet; the next circle of skydivers will open at 3,000 feet; the next row opens at 2,500 feet; and the last outside ring opens at 2,000 feet. In

Jerry Bird's team put together this 21-way star over Zephyrhills, Florida. Large formations require just as much planning for the separation and opening as for building the star itself. (Carl Boenish)

addition to providing extra free-fall and canopy separation in the sky, the staggered openings prevent a huge canopy traffic jam near the ground with everybody arriving at the same time in the same area.

One of the early jumpers who promoted relative work was Bob Buquor, an outstanding free-fall photographer and jumper. He was particularly interested in the star formations (actually a ring of jumpers holding hands, but we still call it a star). The largest star he ever filmed was a seven-man star shortly before he drowned in the Pacific Ocean during a camera jump. The first eight-man star was recorded a few months later on October 15, 1965.

When an award system for relative work was established by Bill Newell in 1967, it was named the *Bob Buquor Star Crest* and Newell designed the award patch with an eight-way star. To be a Star Crest Recipient (SCR) you must participate in a free-fall star formation containing eight or more skydivers in a completed circle, held together for a minimum of five seconds or 1,000 feet. In July 1971 Newell set up the Star Crest Solo (SCS) emblem for participants who enter a star eighth or later.

Another person whose name is synonymous with relative work activities is Jerry Bird, who has participated in most milestones in RW since the 1960's. For those who would like to read more about relative work, I recommend Pat Work's book, *The Art of Freefall Relative Work*.

To many sport parachutists the art of free-falling is the major enjoyment; the canopy descent is a necessary requirement. You might compare them to people who enjoy diving more than swimming. For them swimming out of the pool is merely a requirement after each dive in order to complete the cycle. The same attitude can apply to skydivers who enjoy the delayed free falls, but not particularly the parachute descent and landing. A significant number of jumpers consider the jump over when the ripcord is pulled. To them, the real thrill and pleasure come with the weightlessness and aerial maneuvering during the actual skydive. But during the last decade, with the development of high-performance square canopies, more and more skydivers have found that the canopy descent can be a lot of fun.

By the mid-1970's, when the square canopies had taken over the sport, at least among the more experienced skydivers, a few people around the country —mainly in Florida, New York, and California—were experimenting with canopy relative work (CRW). No longer were jumpers content just to ride their canopies to the ground. Because the ram-air, square design has good forward speed and maneuverability, it can be flown in formation with other similar designs. It was inevitable that as jumpers flew closer and closer under the canopies, they would try making contact of some kind. At first, that's all it was—contact of

In the Seventies, the square ram-air inflated canopies revolutionized sport parachuting. Canopies are "flown" much like a slow-flying airplane. Forward speeds of 30 mph can be reduced to zero for gentle landings. (Para-Flite, Inc.)

Canopy Relative Work (CRW) came into being with the development of the square ram-air canopies. Interestingly, the stacks are "built" from the bottom rather than the top. The lower parachutist flies gently into the docking position on the knees of the parachutist above. By the end of the Seventies, canopy stacks of more than a dozen parachutes had been recorded. (Phil Rogge, USAPT)

"some kind." The first contacts were "side docks," in which a jumper simply reached out and grabbed the side of the canopy of the person below. The problem was that when the approach was from directly above and behind the canopy below, turbulence made it impossible to make a smooth contact. For a few years, there were various attempts and some contacts but little came of them.

Some skydivers in the De Land, Florida, area were experimenting with CRW as early as 1975, with some success, but 1977 saw CRW take hold from coast to coast. With the work documented by photographs, three-stacks were built in Florida early in 1977; in Stormville, New York, in June 1977; and in Antioch, California, just a few days later.

Then, in August 1977 Steve Haley and Norton Thomas, along with others jumping at Perry Stevens's Antioch Drop Zone in California, made a revolutionary discovery. Avoiding the turbulence that comes off the back of a ram-air canopy, they experimented with docking from below in the clean air underneath the canopy. It was a simple idea that unlocked the whole world of canopy relative work. Although two- or even three-stacks might be accomplished from above, they were rare, and the possibility of larger stacks was almost zero.

An interesting phenomenon often observed during climb to jump altitude is the cat-napping. Loads of 40 or more parachutists will drop off into a sort of hibernation during the ascent. A few minutes before jump altitude, they begin slowly to stir as they check equipment, put on gloves or helmets, and prepare to exit. (Bud Sellick)

By using the reverse order of docking in the smooth air below, the sizes of the canopy stacks became limited only by the amount of working time under the canopy.

Again, time is altitude, whether under an inflated canopy or in free fall. Attempting to make a canopy dock below 1,000 feet is flirting with disaster: collapsed canopies are not uncommon in CRW attempts, and above 1,000 feet the collapsed canopy has time to reinflate. Ironically, Tom Courbat, who could be considered the Father of CRW, broke his own rule while attempting to close number five on a four-stack that was less than 300 feet off the ground. He also broke his neck and suffered assorted other injuries. He was presented an honorary *Canopy Crest Recipient* (CCR) award in his hospital bed but later was back in the air to earn it for real. Courbat's period of recuperation was a boon to the CRW enthusiast because it was during this time that he and the Know-Sense Team from the Antioch Drop Zone created the entire concept for the sport. Courbat wrote articles about CRW and, along with other pioneers, originated the CRW awards system. He administered the program during the tough formative years as CRW Promotions, before turning it over to USPA in January 1980.

There is nothing on earth to compare with the beauty and serenity of a formation building above the clouds. (Carl Boenish)

The *Four-Stack Recipient* is for participating in a canopy stack of at least four canopies; the *Canopy Crest Recipient* (CCR) award is for participating in an eight-stack or larger, held for at least one minute; the *Canopy Crest Soloist* (CCS) award is earned by entering eighth or later in a canopy stack held for at least one minute.

Interestingly enough, once it was proven that a canopy could be used in relative work, some of the round canopies of the Para-Commander type were successfully used in CRW. Combination round and square canopies have also been used together.

The new, exotic parachute designs that allow greater comfort and greater control may make the descent and landing more fun for the present generation of skydivers, but to many of the old-timers who have descended in nonsteerable canopies into thorn trees, rock quarries, rivers, and power lines, there is a certain amount of fatherly tolerance for those who will never know what they missed. Like those war experiences, they are nice to reminisce about, but hell to live through at the time.

And to clear up any misunderstandings about who are the old-timers, they are those who jumped in pre-Para-Commander days. Many of the most famous have been defrocked now by a generation that isn't satisfied with jump stories or impressed with past performances. Like some of our heroes of American history who have been reduced to mere mortals with human weaknesses, some of our heroes of sport parachuting in America have even been accused and abused.

The entire sport probably owes more to Jacques Istel and Lew Sanborn than to any other men in the history of our sport. However, when they made it a profession and dared charge a fee for qualified instruction and quality sport parachuting equipment, they were subjected to abuse and accused of profiteering. For years there was a feeling about parachuting that bordered on the divine. Those few who were recognized as experts in the sport held godlike power over the masses, even though they didn't necessarily seek that power. Those days and those men are gone, for the most part, although a few have withstood the test of time. Several survivors now manufacture equipment or sell or operate successful professional parachute centers.

Today there are hundreds of excellent sport parachute clubs or centers with skilled, competent skydivers anxious to instruct and assist the novice. Equipment can be purchased or rented at a reasonable cost from many sources. Anyone who wants to learn the sport of skydiving or even make "just one parachute jump to see what it's like" will have no trouble locating competent instructors and quality equipment. Skydiving has become a full-fledged, respectable, recognized sport.

6. Pour le Sport

Competition and Sport Jumping

By the time you have achieved the degree of competency to be able to control your emotions (to think clearly under extremely foreign situations) and control your body (to respond quickly and accurately), you will be ready to take command of your equipment. You have determined your own ability and limitations during your training and early free-fall experience. Now you will learn the limitations and characteristics of your equipment. Today's equipment is so highly refined that you will make new discoveries every time you get together with skydivers from a different drop zone than yours. You will find that relative workers want one kind of rig while accuracy jumpers prefer another. Large people prefer different outfits than small people. Some will wear a hard helmet, some will wear a soft one, and some won't wear one at all! And on the other end

When the Security piggyback assembly was introduced in 1964, having the main and reserve both on the back was quite an innovation. By those standards it was compact, taking up little more space than earlier backpacks alone, but was very heavy. (Ralph White)

Carl Boenish (left) and Jim Handbury, both wearing the Handbury Rig parachute assembly, demonstrate the state of the art in light, compact parachutes. Looking more like half-empty hiker's backpacks, these are complete rigs with both main and reserves. Performance is more than twice as good as the older rigs but the total weight is less than half as much. (Bud Sellick)

are boots, sneakers, rubber thongs, and a few bare feet. The jumpsuits, which cost more now than the entire rig cost ten years ago, are large, larger, largest, and enormous. Some of those jumpsuits are even ram-air inflated like some canopies. But many of the style jumpers, particularly, are going back to less bulky jumpsuits. So all you can be certain of regarding equipment is that it keeps changing and keeps getting more expensive.

Because change is so rapid in the sport of parachuting, I won't go into detail on the equipment being used. You will learn about that when you visit the parachute centers and talk with active skydivers. But there are a few comments that will give you a better understanding of the equipment used. Headgear, footgear, and jumpsuits are important, but the parachute canopy is the main concern. Actually two parachute canopies are of major concern, since you will always carry a reserve in the event the main malfunctions.

Until the late 1950's parachutes remained pretty much the same as they were when Leonardo da Vinci sketched the first design in 1495. The canopy was usually round, although some square canopies were seen occasionally, and it acted as a drag to slow the rate of descent. Originally it was intended only to save the jumper's life when death was otherwise certain. Therefore, no thought was given to the discomfort of opening shock and little thought to the agony of a few broken bones from landing. The soul purpose was to get you from up there to down here alive. If you landed alive and uninjured as well, so much the better. Back in 1919 Leslie Irvin broke his leg making the world's first free-fall parachute jump, which was considered an unqualified success. His parachute companies around the world—including Irvin Aerospace Industries, which has been heavily involved with space recovery systems—attest to that success. Forty years later I broke my leg making my first free-fall parachute jump in essentially the very same parachute. Like Irvin, I considered it an unqualified success . . . I was still alive. With those flat, circular, nonsteerable parachutes, it was a toss-up which hurt more, the opening shock or the impact with the ground. Obviously, those of us who jumped intentionally from a perfectly good airplane were eyed with dismay . . . among other nouns. There was little chance for a sport to develop until somebody came up with a better parachute canopy.

Round canopies were modified with slots and holes, which allowed air to escape and push the canopy forward, giving some degree of control. Steering was done by pulling down on risers or lines to warp the canopy and deflect the air. Then steering lines were added to make it easier. Sleeves were invented to slow the opening sequence, making the opening more reliable while greatly reducing the opening shock. At last parachute jumping was becoming less painful and more fun.

In the 1950's, when enough people around the world had become "sport parachutists," World Parachuting Championships were established. In the 1960's Lemoigne's para-sail type canopies (the Para-Commander and its many variations), Rogallo's delta-shaped designs (Parawing, Thunderbow, etc.), and the Barish Sailwing all contributed to the growth of the sport. But Domina Jalbert's parafoil design, which hit the sport parachuting market in the 1970's, was truly revolutionizing. This ram-air inflated fabric airfoil actually created lift just as an airplane wing did. Terminology had to change with this square design, which is actually "flown" rather than "jumped" like a conventional parachute. Because it generates up to 30 mph forward speed, light winds were no longer a problem, yet feather-light touchdowns were possible with pinpoint accuracy. What the Para-Commander designs were to the 1960's, the parafoil designs were to the 1970's. Reserve canopies have followed this same revolutionary track. Steerable reserves are both round or square and pack up into increasingly smaller units.

With this brief history of the development of sport parachutes, let's take a quick look at the development of competition. For more details on results, rules, and regulations, refer to the Appendix. Space does not permit coverage of all the national and international events, obviously, but here are some of the highlights.

Competition parachute jumps in the United States go back to 1926, when the first "championship" was held as an extra event at the Pulitzer Air Races in Philadelphia. Joe Crane, a parachute jumper himself, initiated and ran the event. During this event he organized the jumpers into the National Parachute Jumpers-Riggers Association. (NPJR was reorganized in 1957, by Joe Crane and Jacques

In the late Fifties, military surplus parachutes were modified for sport; portions of the canopy were removed and short steering lines were attached. They were cheap to buy (as low as $15 per canopy) and referred to as "cheapos" (bottom, left). A little later came the "sport parachute," which was still a flat circular with portions removed, but was more colorful and was manufactured from low-porosity nylon. It was called a "lo-po." We still had a long way to go. (Joe Gonzales, U.S. Army)

Competition and Sport Jumping 159

The ram-air inflated "square" canopy has dominated the sport since the early Seventies. Accuracy landing is made into the wind with gentle touchdown. Although for experienced jumpers only, the parachute is much lighter and more reliable than any others. However, it does not settle like a standard parachute and must be "flown" to the target. The XL Cloud seen here is the model for the Eighties. (Para-Flite, Inc.)

In the Sixties, the Para-Commander was truly a sport parachute and revolutionized the sport. Accuracy was good, provided the landing was downwind. You speared the target with your toe and you streaked past it. Regardless of how close to the target, every downwind landing was a "crash-and-burn." Landing into the wind was more tolerable but accuracy was erratic. (U.S. Air Force)

Istel, as the Parachute Club of America, forerunner of today's United States Parachute Association.) At the 1926 meet, and in succeeding meets, the jumpers participated in "spot jumping contests" to see who could land closest to the "spot." With jump-and-pulls being done from very slow and very low airplanes, the person who got out and opened the parachute over the "spot" was sure to be the person who landed closest to it. (It is from those activities that we get the term "spotting," determining the opening point over the target in today's accuracy jumps.) For the next 25 years these were the only parachuting contests held in the United States, although other countries around the world were having similar events.

In 1951 the First World Parachuting Championship was held in Bled, Yugoslavia. All seventeen competitors—fifteen men and two women—competed in the three accuracy events. They all wore nonsteerable, flat circular type parachutes. Only five countries participated—the United States didn't. But the Second World Parachuting Championship in 1954 included one lone American, Sergeant Fred Mason. This second "world" meet had grown to 31 contestants. This time they added the "style" event to the two accuracy jumps. The "style" was a twenty-second delayed free fall, while holding a horizontal face-down position. Don't laugh—holding stable for twenty seconds was quite an accomplishment back then. The openings at terminal must have been tough, too, since there were no such things as sleeves or deployment systems. An interesting note here is that the winner of the accuracy jump was Ivan Fedcisin with an average of 5 meters (about 16 feet) using a Soviet *square* PD-47 canopy. It wasn't the ram-air type square canopy of today but an old flat square canopy that was "controlled" by pulling down on the risers and suspension lines. It had no forward speed but came down very fast.

These "world" events were still pretty small when the Third World Parachuting Championship was held in Moscow in 1956, but the events were becoming more complex. The spot jumps for accuracy remained, as did the style event. But now a team event had been added. The sleeve deployment had been introduced by the Soviets for the delayed jumps, and steerable canopies appeared in the form of slotted canopies. The sport was maturing into real competition.

In 1958 the Fourth WPC was swept by the Soviets with their sleeve-deployed blank gore parachutes; they took both men and women's events in team and individual events. The pace quickened and the Fifth WPC had grown to 137 jumpers from twelve countries. The individual and team accuracy events were increased to four each, all with 30-second delays. American Jim Arender won the gold for first place in style, and another American, Dick Fortenberry, scored the first dead center ever made in world competition, using a Double-L modification.

From 1962, when the Sixth WPC was held, the first in the United States, to 1972, when the Eleventh WPC was held, again in the United States, the competition events remained relatively intact: style and accuracy for men and women and for individuals and teams.

During the late 1960's and early 1970's, relative workers were doing their own thing. They were building ten-way stars and other larger stars and formations. They held their own RW competitions locally and sometimes went to other countries, but RW had not reached WPC levels yet. However, at the 1972 U.S. National Parachuting Championships, the first ten-way star event was held as a USPA-sanctioned part of the competition. Six teams competed in six rounds of competition RW, judged on how fast a team could build a ten-way star. Jerry Bird's All Stars team won with an average of 22.26 seconds to build a full ten-way star. The next year seventeen teams competed in the ten-way star Nationals, and again Jerry Bird's team, Columbine Turkey Farm, took first place with an average time on six jumps of 17.63 seconds. By 1974 RW was a full-fledged segment of the Nationals and Al Krueger's team, Captain Hook and the Sky Pirates, won with a new world record time of 14.78 seconds. The push was on to make RW a part of the World Parachuting Championships.

At the Tenth World Parachuting Championship in Bled, Yugoslavia, only style and accuracy were judged. But Jerry Bird's team, seen here exiting, introduced relative work (RW) to the world parachuting community for the first time. (Carl Boenish)

As far back as 1970, when the United States put together a twelve-man star at the Tenth WPC in Yugoslavia as an exhibition, RW was being promoted at international events around the world. The RW teams were putting on some very good shows for at least five years before they achieved world recognition. Finally, in 1975, the First World Parachuting Championship of Relative Work was held in Warendorf, West Germany. The decision was made to continue to hold WPC for Style and Accuracy in even-numbered years and to add WPC for RW in the odd-numbered years. By now, the sport of parachuting had grown too large to be contained within a few weeks every other year on the international level.

Because the sport is changing so rapidly, it would be almost foolhardy for me to try to explain the various events and competition rules. By the time you have reached the level of skill where you are ready to enter the competition, you won't be getting your information from textbooks. But for the interested person who would like to know just a little more about the competitive aspects of skydiving, let's take a quick look at the events.

Dwight Reynolds pushes the 4-inch target into the pea gravel for one of his more than 1,000 dead-center landings. He won the Men's World Accuracy record with 105 dead-center landings without a miss! A member of the U.S. Army Parachute Team, he is co-holder of six world team accuracy records. (Phil Rogge, USAPT)

Cheryl Stearns has won more national and world parachuting championships and holds more records than any woman in history. She holds the Women's Night World Parachute Accuracy record with 23 dead centers. In the style event, she holds the Women's World Style Record with a 6.3-second style series and won the Women's Over All World's Champion title in 1978. A licensed pilot with multiple ratings, she is the first woman to be a member of the U.S. Army Parachute Team. Her next goal is to win the World's Aerobatic Flying championship. (Phil Rogge, USAPT)

Accuracy events, originally spot jumping events, have been with us since the very first contests were held. The idea is for the parachutist to touch the center of a target, usually a 4-inch plastic disc. Obviously, the higher you are above the target area, the more skill it takes to hit the target. To get an idea of what is involved, try dropping clothespins into a tin can at your feet first, then try dropping them into the same tin can from the top of a ten-story building.

With the old nonsteerable parachutes you landed wherever the wind blew you. Spot jumping was a guessing game of how far upwind to jump in order to drift to the target on landing. Of course, if the wind was unsteady, the guessing was pretty unreliable. Then, as steerable canopies reached the sport, there was less room for error because the accuracy jumper could steer into the wind or with the wind to go farther or shorter during the drift to the ground. Finally the

Jimmy Lowe, during a style series, initiates the left turn. (Carl Boenish)

ram-air square canopies eliminated all the guesswork. At the 1976 National Parachuting Championships, for example, at the end of the ten regulation accuracy jumps, ten contestants were tied for first place with ten dead centers each! Finally, fifteen rounds later, Frank Poynter and Ron Walker were tied for first place with 25 dead centers each. In Round 26 Poynter beat Walker by one centimeter (that's less than half an inch!) to win first place. Walker, with 25 dead centers and one 4-centimeter jump, came in second. Debbie Schmidt was the first woman to score dead center on all ten rounds in a National meet. There were 528 dead centers scored in all, so it was obvious that accuracy events required expert marksmen from then on. Scoring for the accuracy events starts at zero and you are awarded a point for each centimeter away from the 4-inch disc. If you miss the disc by 15 centimeters, your score is 15. At the end of ten rounds you total the points "earned" during the ten jumps. As in golf, the lower the score, the better.

Style events were originally nothing but stable, face-to-earth free falls. They are subject to rule changes, like any event, but currently involve some complicated free-fall maneuvering. During free fall, the stylist tucks into a tight position to fall fast but stable. When the contestant starts the first turn, judges start their stopwatches and time how long it takes the contestant to complete the international series. The series consists of a 360-degree circle in one direction followed immediately by 360 degrees in the opposite direction. Next is a backloop, and then two more 360-degree circles in opposite directions followed by a second backloop. As a competitor, you would be saying to yourself as you execute the maneuvers, "Left turn, right turn, backloop, right turn, left turn, backloop, pull!" The judges stop their watches when you pull your ripcord. Winners complete this international series in seven seconds or less. Again, the shortest time wins.

Spectators on the ground without optics find this event a little boring since they seldom see anything until the parachute opens. Those with optics won't see much more. Judges have to be more skilled than contestants to catch the minute penalties for overshooting and undershooting. Video has come to the rescue recently to assure accurate scoring in this event, because of instant replay.

Style and accuracy events are the classic events that have been part of competition since 1954. In the 1970's various relative work team events were added to the competitions. Following are some of these RW events.

Ten-way speed star. Ten people exit the aircraft and form a ten-person star (all holding hands in a circle, which does not have to be symmetrical). The object is to form the circle in the shortest possible time. Originally the rules

A ten-way star trails smoke for the opening ceremonies of the U.S. Nationals in 1972. (Carl Boenish)

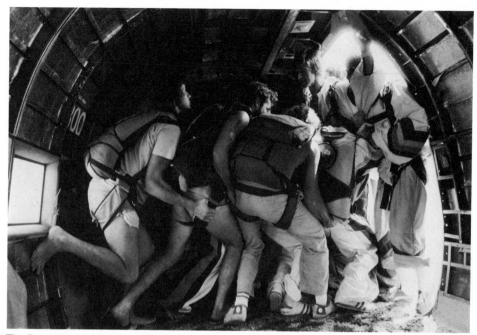

The British team "Symbiosis" practicing their team exit from the DC-3 at Zephyrhills Parachute Center, scene of the World Parachuting Championships of Relative Work in 1981. (Paul Proctor)

stated that the jumpers could not be holding hands when they made the exit but they could be holding onto jumpsuits or equipment. Judging was impossible since the mass of bodies tumbling from the jump plane was just a large glob when viewed from the ground, even with optics and video. Finally it was decided that there would be no restriction as far as contacts at exit, if you could jam ten people through the aircraft door while all holding hands, more power to you. Actually, holding hands is not necessary but you must have a "grip" somewhere between the elbow and fingertips. As in the individual style event, the shortest time to complete the maneuver is the best score. Remember, these ten people are wearing two parachutes each. Jamming ten people and twenty parachutes through that aircraft door is some trick in itself. The speed star has probably done more to influence the size and shape of parachute equipment than anything in the history of jumping.

Eight-way and four-way sequential events. This can be any number but currently the eight-way and four-way are the most popular and are used in WPC of RW. As in the speed star event, time is important both in exiting the aircraft and in RW outside the aircraft. The contestants are allotted a certain amount of time, starting from the moment of exit, to perform as many prescribed formations as possible. The eight (or four) skydivers execute formations in sequence until time runs out and parachutes are opened. The type of formations required are illustrated in the Appendix.

There's more to sport jumping than competing to be more accurate or to turn faster or to build faster stars or faster sequentials. There are a lot of jumps that are made just for fun. At many places around the country there are events, called "boogies," that have no purpose except fun jumping. Most of the time the fun is getting as many people as possible into a very large airplane and then all piling out en masse at 15,000 feet. The group has dirt-dived the jump before loading up so there is still some organization and planning to what may appear to be total chaos. During the National Parachuting Championships for the past several years, the boogie is the place to let down your hair and try something different after weeks of hard training and intense competition.

Some of the less experienced relative workers have decided to try for as big a star as they can build. This is safe enough since all have some RW experience and are getting pretty good, although not yet of competitive stature. Now is the time for them to give it a shot without worrying about messing things up for the other skydivers. The star has built to eleven when one of the RW jumpers breaks into a slot just a little short. Reaching as far as possible, he manages to get

Everybody wants to fun-jump in the boogie, particularly at the U.S. Nationals. A simple fracture acquired during competition won't keep this girl grounded as she registers. (Bud Sellick)

Loading up the DC-3's for the annual boogie jumps at the U.S. Nationals. This is the time to relax and enjoy noncompetitive jumping. (Bud Sellick)

An eight-way Double Donut formation over Casa Grande, Arizona, from the movie *Wings*. (Ray Cottingham)

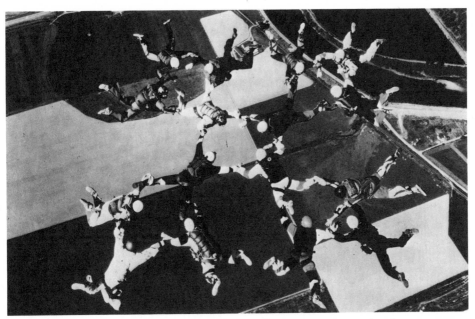

A sixteen-way Quadrupod over Snohomish, Washington. (Ray Cottingham)

a grip with both hands. The reach increases the drag, however, and he rises above the others. Still hanging on tightly, he flips over the top and is now upside down inside the circle. In the inverted position he is now pulling the others in after him and going down fast. The whole round star is warped and tipped vertically. It twists in the middle as the star begins to funnel. The bottom jumpers have stolen the air of the skydivers above and instantly the formation falls into one tight ball of flailing bodies, still linked together, still fighting to get the big circle righted. The ball finally explodes into a dozen separate pieces. Each individually flopping, spinning, inverted body rights itself and tracks rapidly outward until the pull.

There are plenty of other contests for skydivers that are not as competitive as National or World meets, yet they are fun and different. There are the POPS (Parachutists Over Phorty Society) contests, for example. One of the events is the Hit and Rock event. After hitting as close to the target as possible, the contestant jumps into a rocking chair and rocks! This is a takeoff on the old Hit and Run event in the 1950's and 1960's. The idea then was to land on the target, which was a bell. Nobody then ever landed *on* the target so the jumpers tried to land as close as they could, but always upwind. They were timed from the time they hit the ground until they rang the bell. If they landed downwind, they would nearly always have to take off the parachute harness to run upwind and ring the bell; but if they landed downwind, they could leave the harness and parachute on and trot downwind easily with the wind pulling them to the target to ring the bell.

A number of Para-Ski contests are held each year, combining skills in both parachute jumping and skiing. The rules are varied but basically the object is to land at a point near your skis, and the 4-inch target, pull off the parachute and put on the skis, then race against the clock down a giant slalom course.

Some other fun jumps don't require anything more than originality. Here's one for hang glider enthusiasts. After ejecting themselves from a hang glider piloted by Rich Piccarilli, jumpers Jim Handbury and Brian Johnson made a quick RW hookup before opening their parachutes. The three had launched off Half-Dome Peak in Yosemite National Park on July 3, 1977.

Speaking of hookups, how's this for being creative? In June 1976 three test jumpers—Mark Malick, Hoot Gibson, and Larry Krueger—were testing reserves when they took the opportunity to do something a little different in the way of RW. They exited at 7,500 feet testing North American Aerodynamics' lightweight piggyback reserves. They did a quick three-man hookup and held it for five seconds, then broke apart and deployed the main parachutes. After repositioning themselves under the open canopies, they cut away simultaneously at 6,000 feet. Back in free fall, they flew together at 4,200 feet for the first "relative work cutaway three-man star" ever created. They broke at 3,500 feet and opened their reserves. It's nice to see people enjoy their work.

Of course, there are always those who get tired of jumping out of airplanes and try parachuting from earthbound structures. These jumpers claim that with careful planning and preparation, their jumps are as safe as any from planes. The authorities who arrest them are not in total agreement with this philosophy. In July 1975, Owen Quinn jumped off the top of the 110-story World Trade Center's North Tower in New York City. Thousands of afternoon commuters watched as he floated down. He landed safely at the plaza level but suffered minor injuries to both legs. Police escorted him to Bellevue Hospital for observation. A few years later George Willig, the mountain climber, climbed up the tower and became a hero. Evidently, climbing up is heroic but jumping off is insane.

A year after making their skydives off El Capitan, four of the "El Cap" skydivers were searching for another jumping-off place. In August 1979, John Noak, David Blattel, Robin Heid, and Carl Boenish leaped from the Royal Gorge Bridge west of Canyon City, Colorado. They were arrested immediately but after a four-hour search turned up no law against parachuting off the bridge, they were released. The police, the mayor, and the townspeople were all very courteous, according to the four daring divers. Nine years earlier, Don Boyles did a free-fall solo off the same bridge wearing a surplus Double-L canopy.

And speaking of bridge-jumping, Roger Worthington, celebrating his eleventh year of skydiving, became the first man to parachute from the 244-foot high Coronado Bridge over San Diego Bay. Six months later he parachuted off the 450-foot-high Pine Valley Bridge near San Diego.

SAFETY RULES

Because there are certain dangers involved in any active sport, rules of safety are set up within the ranks to govern that sport. Parachuting for sport owes its very survival to a number of persons who set up basic rules for self-regulation. Nobody likes to be restricted by regulations or rules, so often "doctrine" or "suggestions" is used. Whatever we call them, rules of safety are necessary. Where dangerous parachuting was conducted before any rules existed, states passed regulations forbidding parachute jumps. Every time a parachutist spattered the countryside, laws were passed to further restrict parachuting. There was no distinction made between safe jumping and dangerous jumping; to the uninformed, all parachute jumping was dangerous. Through education of the public and the legislators, anti-parachuting laws were repealed or changed to comply with those standards of safety and conduct set up by the parachutists themselves. Through the efforts of Jacques Istel, who gave very persuasive talks—backed up by actual demonstrations before state and federal aviation authorities—sport parachuting gained the respectability it needed to survive and prosper.

Until the 1960's, the Federal Aviation Administration did not recognize a parachutist as a human being. The jumper was officially considered "an object" dropped from a plane, and the pilot was held 100 percent responsible for any damage just as surely as if he had dropped a brick. Obviously, pilots were not anxious to be held responsible for the actions of some madman—and most pilots felt that only a madman would jump from a perfectly good airplane—so they were understandably cautious about whom they flew. This accounts for the extremely high percentage of parachutists then who were also pilots. Only a parachutist felt confident of another parachutist's ability, so they frequently flew each other. Now things have changed, and the FAA officially recognizes a parachutist as a person capable of controlling his or her descent in such a way as to land without undue danger either to self or to persons and property on the ground. The current FAA regulations (see Appendix for some of these rules) reflect the influence of parachutists themselves and the official safety rules of the national parachuting organization, USPA. New rules to meet changing equipment capabilities and changing moods of the skydivers are reviewed by the safety and training committee of USPA as the need arises. What was once grounds for revoking a parachutist's license (such as skydiving off El Capitan or the World Trade Center) may be acceptable or even endorsed later when experience and equipment prove the activity safe.

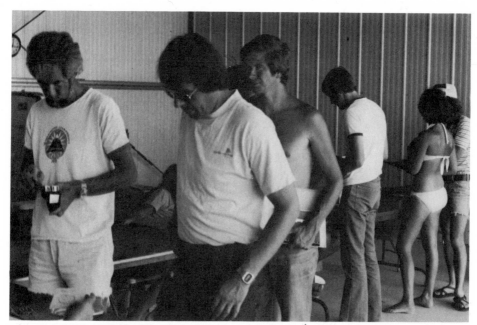

At registration for the U.S. Nationals everybody signs up and pays up before the show gets in the air. (Bud Sellick)

In 1979, at the U.S. Nationals in Richmond, Indiana, video was used for the first time as the "official" scoring system for Style and RW. Two video cameras are trained on the jump plane as the ground control person gives the radio command, "Exit, exit, exit." (Bud Sellick)

Two canopy relative workers make it look easy. (Bud Sellick)

Spectators and contestants congregate in the carnival atmosphere of a typical competition. But everybody packs his or her own parachute. (Bud Sellick)

A DC-3 exit with sunburst is captured on film by expert skydiver-photographer Ray Cottingham. Skydiving activities are every photographer's delight. (Ray Cottingham)

As the pilot chute is released by the base person, everyone will turn 180 degrees and track away for their openings. This is a "still" from the movie *Wings*. (Ray Cottingham)

NIGHT JUMPING

Jumping at night is permissible and safe when done in accordance with FAA and USPA recommendations. This is exhilarating and exciting for both the participants and the spectators on the ground. Sometimes it may get more exciting than was expected. On my first night jump I made a short ten-second delay. The pilot, who had never flown a night jump before, reported to the observers on the ground that he never saw my chute open. This was understandable, because in ten seconds I had dropped more than 1,100 feet below the plane. As was typical in those flat circular, nonsteerable canopy days, I landed in waist-deep water half a mile from the airport. While searchers probed the darkness with flashlights for my mangled body, my wife clung to the hope that somehow I had survived the plunge. When I finally wandered into the hangar an hour after the jump, she was on the verge of hysteria. I explained to the jump pilot that in the future he need not expect to see the parachute open on night parachute jumps.

Looking down from several thousand feet over the countryside at night is a beautiful sight; the tiny lights below give a fairyland appearance to everything. But there are added difficulties in night jumping. Getting an accurate wind drift indicator (WDI) that is lighted and visible during descent is desirable, although it is often lost in the maze of other lights on the ground. A dependable ground crew is a necessity for any jumps, but especially those at night. One of the ground crew should mark the landing point of the WDI with a flashing beacon or other easily recognizable light. Be sure you are looking at the right beacon, however. I once tried to lead a couple of fellow skydivers out over a radio tower beacon two miles from the target. All three of us were poised outside the 182 ready to exit when my friend Bob Vaughn pointed out my error. To add to the fiasco, his flare wouldn't burn so he had set it back on the airplane floor at exit rather than drop it in the dark or carry a worthless flare in his hand. The pilot was a little more than upset when the flare reignited itself on the plane's carpet once it was in out of the slipstream. Good thing we had insurance.

Night jumping should be limited to good weather conditions. Light winds or no wind is best, depending on the type of parachute canopy being used. A bright moon can be very helpful but isn't necessary. A flashlight is both helpful and necessary but if you plan to use the same ground crew again, don't drop it. If you've ever been on the ground at night and heard that terrifying sound of something whistling down out of the darkness, you know that it rates a pucker factor of ten! Safety requires that you display a flashing light on your body so you can be seen by airplanes as well as other skydivers. Getting run over by your jump pilot is no better than getting run over by a perfect stranger. Your flashing light must be visible for at least three miles to be legal and safe.

With the high-performance parachutes used today, night jumps can be

The ten-way speed star "Wings of Orange" on a night jump. (Ray Cottingham)

just as accurate as day jumps, if you can just find the target. Your depth perception will be different, though, and the familiar surroundings often get unfamiliar in the darkness. The target area can be marked with flares, or electric light bulbs. Flares are less desirable since they not only set fires in the grass but burn parachutes and parachutists. The lights should be arranged in a circle with a radius of 25 meters (about 80 feet). Normally the landings are made into the wind. The light closest to the wind line on the downwind side of the target should be turned off to leave an open "gate" into the circle of lights. For added help, a line of three or four lights along the wind line can be set up to lead the skydiver through the opening to the target. For accuracy jumps, a red light can be placed at dead center, covered with Plexiglas flush with the surface. USPA's Part 112 covers doctrine for night jumps, and you should read it before engaging in this type of jumping.

FLARES AND SMOKE BOMBS

Night jumps are sometimes made with flares, day jumps often with smoke. Both provide better viewing by the spectators. However, both can be dangerous and

The U.S. Army Parachute Team exits a UA-1 Otter for a demonstration jump with smoke. After clearing the aircraft, one of the skydivers is about to pull a lanyard, releasing the pins from his smoke bombs attached to his boot heel. (Phil Rogge, USAPT)

should be handled with care. There are a number of commercially produced flares and smoke bombs available to the sport parachutist; also a large number are secured through military sources, often illegally. Although both can be hand-held if properly mounted for that purpose, some get extremely hot, occasionally starting grass fires when dropped. Boot brackets for clamping smoke bombs or flares to the boot are also available, and this is the recommended method of carrying them. A few words of caution regarding boot-mounted smoke bombs and flares: do not bend your legs back in a tight frog position or you may make *yourself* into a flare! Participating in a mass exhibition jump, Larry Estep did not realize he was about to set himself afire during his delayed free fall. On the ground he found that he had burned away a portion of his jumpsuit and badly scorched the saddle of his parachute harness. The boot brackets have also been known to entangle with a deploying parachute during unstable openings. You should be able to remove the bracket quickly in the event of an emergency. The brackets can be as dangerous as the smoke bomb or flare when used by unskilled jumpers. Generally, the use of smoke and flares should be limited to advanced skydivers.

CLOUDS

Although parachuting through clouds has been outlawed by the FAA, there are many of us who feel it should be permitted, possibly because we had been dropping through clouds for years before somebody decided to make it illegal. The danger, of course, is the possibility of collision with an airplane. However, when a medium-sized fluffy cumulus cloud is observed for several minutes and no planes are seen flying near it, there is little chance a plane has taken refuge and is hiding in there. Large cloud banks that cover a significant area of the sky are another story, but there is a special enjoyment that comes with picking out a lonely little cumulus cloud and then leaping into it as though it were a big featherbed.

On one particular high jump with demonstration partner Jim Thompson, we exited at 18,000 feet, above scattered clouds that were topping at about 6,000 feet. We found that our fall was carrying us into a rather large cloud, so we maintained stable fall to prevent collision. After we had fallen two miles toward the clouds, they suddenly took on the appearance of solid bodies. For a split second, I had the sensation of impacting a solid surface as Jim and I struck the cloud with a poof. The cloud was thin and light and we were quickly out again, but falling through several thousand feet of cloud can result in total disorientation.

Another time I carried a hand-held smoke bomb into a cloud that extended from a base at 3,000 feet to a rolling dome at 10,000 feet and growing. Starting from 12,000 feet, I entered the top of the cloud in about fifteen seconds and descended through a light gray mist. Holding a modified stable spread position, I tried to keep track of my instruments, but water vapor condensed on both instruments and goggles, making reading difficult. As I wiped the goggles and instruments with a gloved hand, I could see that my smoke was no longer trailing up but was trailing back over my right shoulder. Then it was streaming directly sideways from my left hand across in front of my face and past my right hand. Although I had no sensation of falling, it was obvious I was falling on one side. From then on, I turned my body in relation to the streaming smoke and kept it flowing straight up from the bomb. Near the base of the cloud formation the light gray turned to dark gray and finally to nearly complete darkness. I broke through the bottom of the cloud as though dropping through a trap door. After I opened my parachute I realized that I was damp all over. The air was noticeably muggy and hot compared to the cool trip through the cloud.

Like jumping at night, jumping through a cloud is a unique experience. I wish everyone could experience it at least once.

Using hand-held smoke to keep him oriented, the author drops into a heavy cloud before regulations prohibited cloud-jumping. (Bud Sellick)

WATER JUMPING

Jumping into water offers some unique advantages and hazards. Many of us who have broken a few bones here and there in the sport have found that water jumps afford a means of resuming jumping before a complete recovery.

Mari-Lou MacDonald, a Canadian women's parachute champion, broke her back while skydiving, but fourteen months later she dived into the cool blue air over Toronto and drifted lazily down into her target area in the water beside the Canadian National Exhibition. It is best to wait until the casts have been removed. Experience has taught me that wet casts are soon reduced to mushy plaster and long trails of gauze. Some have tried waterproofing their casts with rubber inner tubes or plastic bags, but few have been successful at it.

Regardless of the physical condition of the parachutist who is making a water jump, he or she should observe certain basic safety rules. Adequate flotation gear must be worn regardless of swimming ability. The military life preservers designed for pilots are excellent, since they can easily be worn under the parachute and then quickly inflated by CO_2 cartridges when needed. Shorts, T-shirt, and sneakers are adequate clothing under normal summertime conditions. Pat Catherwood, Dave Hillis, and Bill Hardman of Abbotsford, B.C., jumped into the Pacific Ocean on New Year's Day, 1970, to publicize the Fiftieth

Intentional water jumps are fun when properly planned and executed. A motorboat and at least two swimmers are required. This jumper has released his harness straps and will drop free the moment his feet strike the water. (Joe Gonzales, U.S. Army)

Annual Polar Bear Club New Year's Day swim. Although the water was reported at 42 degrees, the three survived to claim the year's first water jumps.

In an intentional water landing, it's best to avoid instruments which are difficult to keep dry. On long delays you will have to wear an altimeter but this can be easily stowed in a waterproof plastic bag and tucked into a pocket. Don't forget that if you are jumping with only a bathing suit and sneakers, your rate of descent will be faster than when you wear a jumpsuit. Immediately after opening, the reserve on conventional rigs should be released to one side of the harness. Many people don't like to get their best parachute gear wet so water jumps are often the scene of equipment out of the closet. Depending on the type of life preserver you are wearing, you can inflate it immediately after opening or wait until you are closer to the water and have released your chest strap and other hardware. Just sit back in the saddle and wait until you reach the water. The type of life preserver and the type of harness you are wearing will determine the exact procedures, so be sure to have a dry run on the ground before jumping to familiarize yourself with them. Some types of inflation gear can be inflated while you are wearing the harness and some can't.

Safety requires a motorboat containing two or more people with face mask and swim fins and a knowledge of life-saving procedures. See USPA's Part 113 for doctrine on intentional water jumps.

EMERGENCY JUMP SITUATIONS

Water landings. Intentional water jumps are safe when carefully planned and properly executed. But sometimes a water jump is unintentional. This is an extremely serious situation for even the most expert of swimmers. Assuming you have no flotation gear and are fully clothed for a normal landing on terra firma, you should immediately begin preparing for a water landing if there is a 50–50 chance of getting wet. If you're wearing a chest-mounted reserve, unsnap it and release it to one side. Get back in the saddle of your harness if you have that type. Discard helmet, gloves, and boots if wearing them. Giving up expensive equipment is hard to do but your life may be at stake; many who gambled on keeping the gear are dead now—as many as a third of the fatalities in the sport are drownings. Get free from as much of your harness as you can before reaching the water, but don't release everything until your feet are wet (people have misjudged the distance above water and released as much as 200 feet above the surface, which can be just as fatal as drowning). Once in the water you may want to hang onto your harness if the wind is blowing toward the shore. It could pull you to shallow water. Otherwise release it and get away from it before you become entangled in it. A jumpsuit will make an excellent life preserver once it's wet. A wet jumpsuit will hold air if you blow into it and prevent the air from escaping around your collar. Otherwise take it off and

Unintentional water landings can be extremely dangerous. You must get rid of all equipment before reaching the water, then get free of the harness the moment you enter. If the wind is blowing toward the shore, you can keep the canopy inflated and hang onto the harness, letting it pull you ashore. If the wind is blowing away from the shore, let go of the harness and use your jumpsuit to stay afloat. This jumper is using a seven-separation TU modification "cheapo" canopy. (Joe Gonzales, U.S. Army)

trap as much air in it as possible, then tuck in under your chin and gather your wits before doing anything else. If you keep it wet and periodically force air into it, the suit can keep you up indefinitely, providing adequate flotation until help arrives or until you can work your way to shore.

In August 1967, eighteen jumpers bailed out of a converted World War II B-25 bomber and dropped through clouds (in direct violation of FAA regulations) to discover themselves at least one mile out over Lake Erie. Only Bernard Johnson and Robert Coy survived the tragedy, while sixteen fellow jumpers drowned. The FAA air traffic controller who had been tracking the plane on radar reported the aircraft to be 6 miles inland at the time of the exits. Later investigation, however, indicated some mixup in identification of the jump plane and the photo plane which was to have photographed the jumps. Apparently the photo plane was over the field while the jump plane was over the lake, and their positions on radar were erroneously interpreted. However, if the jumps had not been made over the heavy cloud cover, the jumpers would have seen that they were over water and would not have jumped.

This was one of those cases where you may get away with one small violation of safety, but the odds go up with each additional infraction. Most of the jumpers who drowned could have saved themselves by discarding equipment and inflating their jumpsuits even though they had no flotation gear but, according to Johnson and Coy, there were a number of boats in the immediate area and the jumpers expected these craft to help rescue them. Instead, one large cruiser moved lazily among the floundering parachutists and then turned and headed away, leaving them to drown. By the time many realized the boat was not coming to aid them, they had become too exhausted to discard their equipment and were dragged under. Boots, helmet, and instruments total about $400. Parachutes could run as much as $2,000 or more. With a total of $2,500 worth of equipment, even in an emergency there is a strong resistance to throwing it all away, if there is a remote chance of saving it. In this case, the remote chance was the few boats in the area. It is far better to come back and drag for the equipment than have a rescue squad dragging for a body.

Landing in trees. Landing in trees can be fun and seldom results in injury except to the parachute. When a tree is fully clothed in leaves, it seldom damages even the parachute. This is done later by the jumper who is trying to recover it from the tree. There are two main concerns of the parachutist who is descending into a tree. First, you should avoid coming down near the center of the tree where the branches extend from the trunk and are thick. Rather, aim for the springy outer branches that allow you to drop through but catch the canopy and gently pull you to a stop. Second, you should protect yourself by crossing your arms in front of your face and crossing your legs so you don't straddle a branch. Since you should be wearing goggles, you should be able to keep your eyes open and see what's going on. It is possible to get turned upside down in the branches and drop through head first—a situation to be avoided, particularly if the tree is a small one that would allow the jumper to strike the ground before the canopy is caught.

Power lines. The secret to survival in the event you are being carried into power lines is to avoid touching more than one line at a time. You should look down at the wires and keep your eyes on them so you can kick away and avoid hitting more than one wire. This is one time to throw the ripcord away, if it is being carried on the wrist. (Some ripcords remain in the ripcord housing.) One unfortunate parachutist succeeded in slipping between two wires, touching only one as he went through, but the ripcord on his wrist fell across the other line. Zot! In the event you land upwind of power lines and the canopy blows over the lines, immediately release the canopy from the harness. It will probably continue to glide over the wires and can be retrieved on the other side. If you cannot release the canopy, you must quickly get out of the harness.

Emergency landings are serious, but not necessarily critical. The secret is to be prepared for all emergencies. Practice going through simulated emergencies so they can be quickly coped with at the proper time. The actual emergency is no time to begin practicing! Consider the thousands of lives that have been saved when a pilot made an emergency bailout with all the odds against him or her—and yet survived. It may be of comfort to know that many persons have survived parachute malfunctions with minor injuries. Some have survived serious injuries and returned to jump again.

After all the hairy jump stories that the newcomers are subjected to during the orientation to parachuting, they may be inclined to think their chances of survival are 50–50 at best. Actually, parachuting is as safe as any other similar sport. Safety lies in no single factor, but in a combination of factors. A parachutist must be in good physical and emotional condition to participate safely in the sport, and training and equipment must be good.

Properly conditioned, physically and mentally, a jumper is as safe as the training and equipment. Parachutes seldom fail; it is nearly always the jumper who makes an error. A parachute is as safe as the person who uses it. Like a loaded pistol, a parachute can be a life-saver or a life-taker. A parachute must be treated with respect and care, but not with fear. Nobody can think clearly when filled with terror, so fear must be quickly overcome and replaced with caution. If there is still fear (not to be confused with anxiety) after a dozen or so jumps, the jumper should be encouraged to take up another sport.

Without a doubt, parachuting offers greater freedom of movement than any other sport. To be free as a bird, floating weightlessly through space, is surely unique among all the active sports in the world. There is something unreal about free-falling through space that cannot be adequately described. Only someone who has been there can understand why sport parachuting is addictive. The obstacles to parachuting are many—money, strict governmental regulations, rigid safety standards, fear, and many hours of hard physical labor. Each jump requires time and labor in repacking the parachutes, putting on the equipment and clothing, loading up, and flying to jump altitude—all for a total of only a few minutes of free fall and parachute descent.

To that person who has actually done it, parachuting is the ultimate sport.

Appendix I

World Parachuting Championships of Style and Accuracy

The First World Parachuting Competition, held in Yugoslavia in 1951, was won by France. Only five nations were represented. The second world meet was held in 1954 at St. Yans, France. Army Sergeant Fred Mason was the only U.S. entrant, the first in world competition. The USSR won the meet. In 1956 the Third World Parachuting Championships were held in Moscow and, for the first time, a U.S. team participated. Czechoslovakia placed first; the U.S. sixth. The fourth competition, in Bratislava, Czechoslovakia, in 1958, was won by the USSR.

Number & Year	Place	Overall Men	Overall Women	Men's Team	Women's Team
5th 1960	Sofia, Bulgaria	Czechoslovakia (Kaplan)		USSR	
6th 1962	Orange, Massachusetts	USA (Arender)	USA (Simbro)	Czech	USA
7th 1964	Leutkirch, West Germany	USA (Fortenberry)	USA (Taylor)	Czech	USA
8th* 1966	Leipzig, East Germany	USSR (Krestjannikow)	USSR (Jeremina)	USSR	USSR
9th 1968	Graz, Austria	USSR (Tkatschenko)	USSR (Voinove)	USA	USSR
10th 1970	Bled, Yugoslavia	USSR (Jacmenev)	France (Baulez)	Czech	Czech
11th 1972	Tahlequah, Oklahoma	USA (Schoelpple)	East Germany (Karkoschka)	USSR	USSR
12th 1974	Szolnok, Hungary	USSR (Usmajev)	USSR (Szergejeva)	Czech	USSR
13th 1976	Guidonia, Italy	USSR (Surabko)	USSR (Zakorechkaja)	USSR	USA
14th 1978	Zagreb, Yugoslavia	USSR (Tjorlo)	USA (Stearns)	East Germany	USSR
15th 1980	Kazanluk, Bulgaria	USSR (Usmajev)	East Germany (Walkhoff)	USSR	East Germany

*USA did not permit a team to enter because the event was held in East Germany.

U.S. Men's Team at the Sixth (1962) World Parachuting Championships. Left to right: Phil Vander Weg, Jim Arender, Dick Fortenberry, Gerry Bourquin, Hank Simbro, and Loy Brydon. This was the first World Parachuting Championship held in the United States. (Joe Gonzales)

U.S. Women's Team at the Sixth (1962) World Parachuting Championships. Left to right: Helen Lord, Muriel Simbro, Nona Pond, Gladys Inman, and Carolyn Olson. This team won first place in overall scoring while Muriel Simbro won the Women's Individual World Champion title. (Joe Gonzales)

The U.S. team that competed in the Seventh (1964) World Parachuting Championships at Leutkirch, West Germany. Kneeling, left to right: Maxine Hartman, Tee Taylor (who took first place as Women's World Champion), Carol Penrod, Gladys Inman, Anne Batterson (missing is Susan Clements). Standing, left to right: Team Trainer Captain Charles Mullings, Loy Brydon, Ron Sewell, Coy McDonald, Gerry Bourquin, Bill Berg, Dick Fortenberry (who took first place as Men's World Champion), and team pilot Dave Steeves. The Women's team placed first overall while the Men's team placed third—only 3-1/2 points behind the first-place Czechs. (U.S. Parachuting Association)

The 1966 U.S. National Team did not compete in the Eighth World Parachuting Championships because the meet was held in East Germany. Back row, left to right: Tom Schapanski, Bobby Buscher, Bobby Letbetter (KIA, Vietnam, November 1966), Roy Johnson, Dick Harman, Martine Durbin, Martha Huddleston, Susan Clements, Maxine Hartman. Front row, left to right: Norman Heaton, team leader; Gene Thacker, team coach. (Joe Gonzales)

The 1968 U.S. Team at the Ninth World Championships, Graz, Austria. Back row, left to right: team photographer Chip Maury, head of delegation Charles MacCrone, team leader Lyle Cameron, Gary Lewis, Billy Lockward, Dave Sauve, Jimmy Davis, Clayton Schoelpple. Front row, left to right: FAI judge Gordon Riner, team coach Dick Harman, Karen Roach, Martha Huddleston, Susan Joerns, Barbara Roquemore, Bonnie Hickey (alternate), Annie Zurcher. (Chip Maury)

The 1970 U.S. Parachute Team that competed in the Tenth World Parachuting Championships, Bled, Yugoslavia. Left to right: Suzie Neuman, Doug Metcalfe, Nancy Black, Bill Knight, Barbara Roquemore, Bill Hayes, Susan Rademaekers, Clayton Schoelpple, Gloria Porter, Jim Lowe, Susie Joerns, and Don Rice. (U.S. Parachuting Association)

The 1972 U.S. Parachute Team at Tahlequah, Oklahoma, for the Eleventh World Parachuting Championships. Standing, left to right: Curt Curtis, Ed Fitch, Bob Sprague, Roy Johnson, Charlie Hall, Stan Hicks, Clayton Schoelpple, Tim Saltonstahl, Billy Lockward, and Chuck Collingwood. Kneeling, left to right: (unidentified), Gloria Porter, Lynn McNaughton, Joan Emmack, Susie Joerns, Laura Lockward, Susan Rademaekers, (unidentified). (Cathy Collingwood)

The 1974 U.S. Parachute Team that competed in the Twelfth World Parachuting Championships in Szolnok, Hungary. Standing, left to right: Gene Thacker, Kevin Donnelly, Chuck Collingwood, Jim Lowe, Jack Brake, Stan Hicks, Mickey Bevins. Kneeling, left to right: Linda Miller, Cathy Collingwood, Vikki Herst, Debby Schmidt, and Nancy Black. (USAPT, courtesy Cathy Collingwood)

The 1976 U.S. Parachute Team at Guidonia (Rome), Italy, for the Thirteenth World Parachuting Championships of Style and Accuracy. Standing, left to right: Chuck Collingwood, Jack Brake, Dana Engelstad, Stan Hicks, Jimmy Davis, Roy Hatch, and Jimmy Hayhurst. Kneeling, left to right: Maria Ledbetter, Debby Schmidt, Nancy Wrenn, Perry Hicks, Susie Joerns, and Cheryl Stearns. (USAPT, courtesy Cathy Collingwood)

The 1978 U.S. Parachute Team before selection of final "travel team" that competed in the Fourteenth World Parachuting Championships of Style and Accuracy in Zagreb, Yugoslavia. Back row: Dick Morgan—coach; John Mirus—judge; and Bill Knight—coach. Second row: Jimmy Hayhurst, Mark Limond, Dana Engelstad, Doug Christen, Chuck Whittle —team leader, Roy Hatch, Dwight Reynolds, Dennis Wise, and Bob Von Derau. Front row: Judy Patrick, Cathy Collingwood, Cheryl Stearns, Julie Albritton, Perry Hicks Jordan, Debby Schmidt, Pat Wenger, and Susie Joerns. Not pictured are Maria Johnson and Chuck Collingwood. (USAPT, courtesy Cathy Collingwood)

Appendix II

World Parachuting Championships of Relative Work

Unlike the U.S. National Parachuting Championships, which are held annually in the United States, the FAI (Federation Aeronautique Internationale) sanctioned world championships were held only in even-numbered years. The odd-numbered years were left open for informal international meets or cups, allowing new events to be created and innovations in rules or judging to be tried. World Parachuting Championships consisted of the classical events of style and accuracy.

By the early 1970's, relative work events were being held at national and international cups. The 1972 U.S. Nationals included RW for the first time. The push was on to include RW in the world championships. In 1973 the first FAI-recognized World Cup of RW was held in Elsinore, California. In 1974 another FAI World Cup of RW was held at Pretoria, South Africa, and the decision was made to have World Parachuting Championships of Relative Work on the odd-numbered years rather than try to include RW with the classic events during the regular WPC.

So beginning in 1975, World Parachuting Championships were designated as either Relative Work or Style and Accuracy. 1975 was designated WPC of RW and 1976 was designated WPC of Style and Accuracy. The first WPC of RW in 1975 was held at Warendorf, West Germany, and consisted of a ten-man speed star event and a four-man sequential event. The U.S. team won the ten-way event. In 1977, at the second WPC of RW, in Gatton, Australia, the ten-man speed star was eliminated and the eight-way and four-way sequential events were held. The U.S. team won the gold medal for the eight-way event, while the Canadian team won the four-way with the U.S. placing fourth. The 1979 third WPC of RW at Châteauroux, France, also consisted of the eight-way and four-way speed star. Again the United States took first place in the eight-way event and the Canadian team won the four-way event.

The U.S. four-way and eight-way teams that competed in the Second World Parachuting Championship of Relative Work held at Gatton, Australia, in 1977. Back row, left to right: Roger Hull, judge Lorrie Young, Garry Carter, Mike Eakins, Rande Deluca, Jim Captain, Dave Sheldon, B. J. Worth, and Curt Curtis. Front row, left to right: Dave Wallace, Wilson Rudd, Mike Gennis, G. Hod Sanders, Bungee Wallace, Jim Reilly, and team leader Bill Ottley. (Photo by head of delegation, Dan Poynter)

The Third World Parachuting Championships of Relative Work was held at Châteauroux, France, in 1979. The "Mirror Image" eight-way team took first place gold for the United States. Left to right, back row: Steve Mayes, Mike Gennis, Mike Eakins, Marty Martin, Jerry Bird, and Garry Carter. Front row, left to right: Jim Captain, B. J. Worth, G. Hod Sanders, and Craig Fronk. (Paul Proctor, USPA)

The U.S. four-way team, "Tesseract," at the Third World Parachuting Championships of Relative Work. Left to right: Tim Florea, Jeff Wragg, Brad Dunkin, John Culler, and Ron Urton. (Paul Proctor, USPA)

FOUR-PERSON EVENT SET SEQUENCES

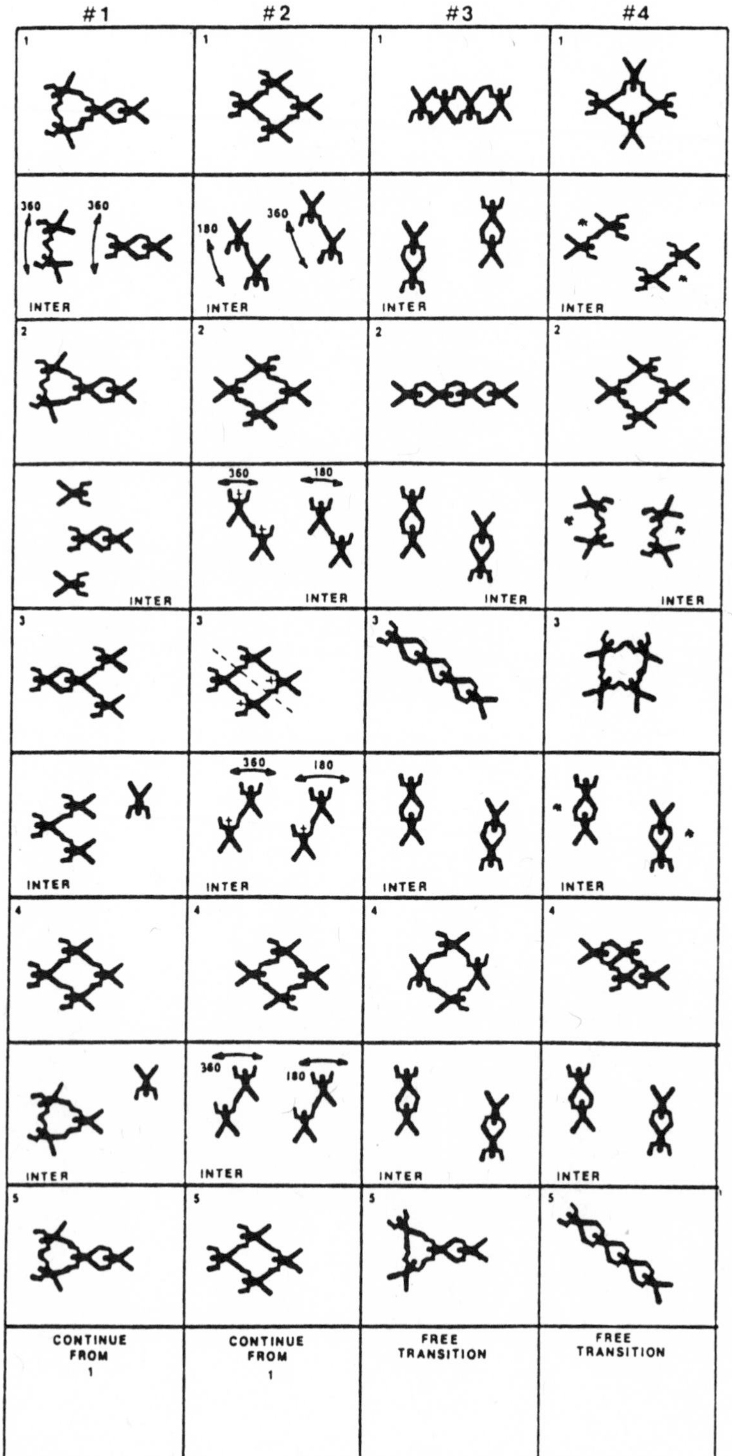

FOUR-PERSON EVENT SET SEQUENCES

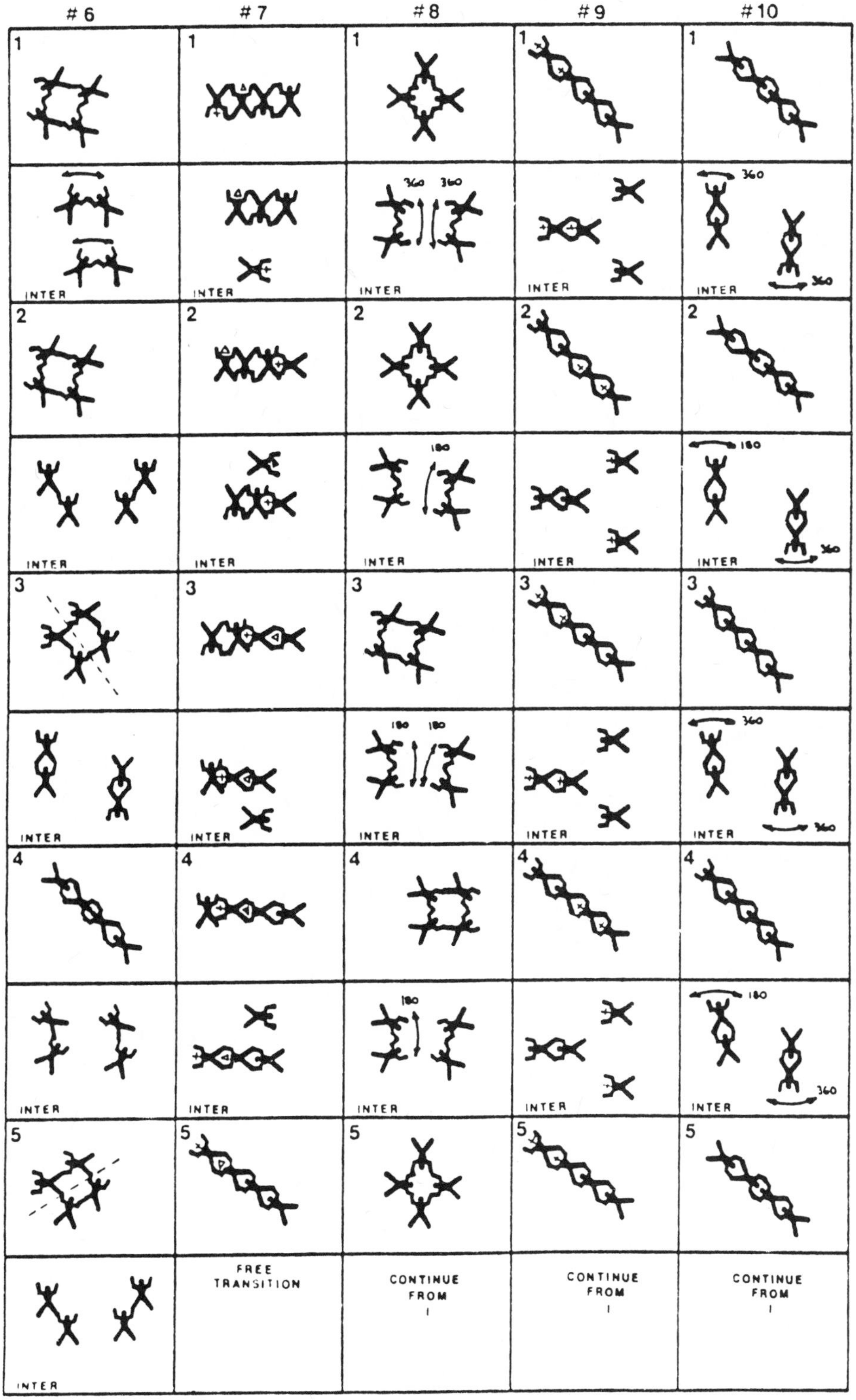

FOUR-PERSON EVENT SET SEQUENCES

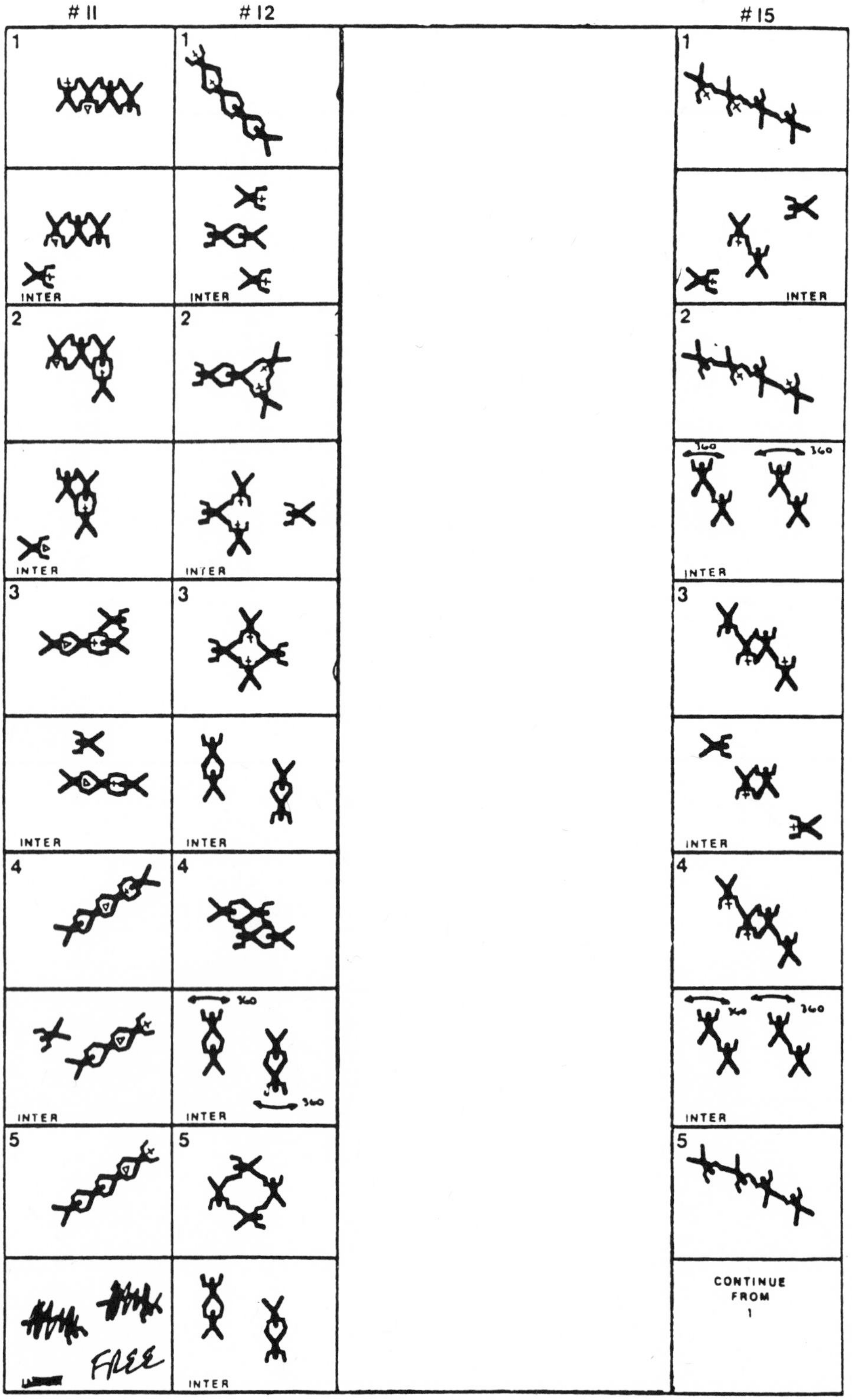

1 STAR	2 SNOWFLAKE	3 BIPOLE	4 DIAMOND	5 DONUT
6 MONOPOD	7 COMPRESSED ACCORDION	8 CATERPILLAR	9 CANADIAN "T"	10 BUNYIP
11 ZIPPER	12 MURPHY		14 STAIRSTEP DIAMOND	15 MARQUIS
16 OFFSET	17 ZIG-ZAG	18 SIDE-FLAKED DONUT	19 "Y"	20 MURPHY FLAKE
21 OPAL	22 UNIPOD		24 OPPOSED DIAMOND	25 ACCORDION

EIGHT-PERSON EVENT   SET SEQUENCES

#5   #6   #7   #8

EIGHT-PERSON EVENT SET SEQUENCES

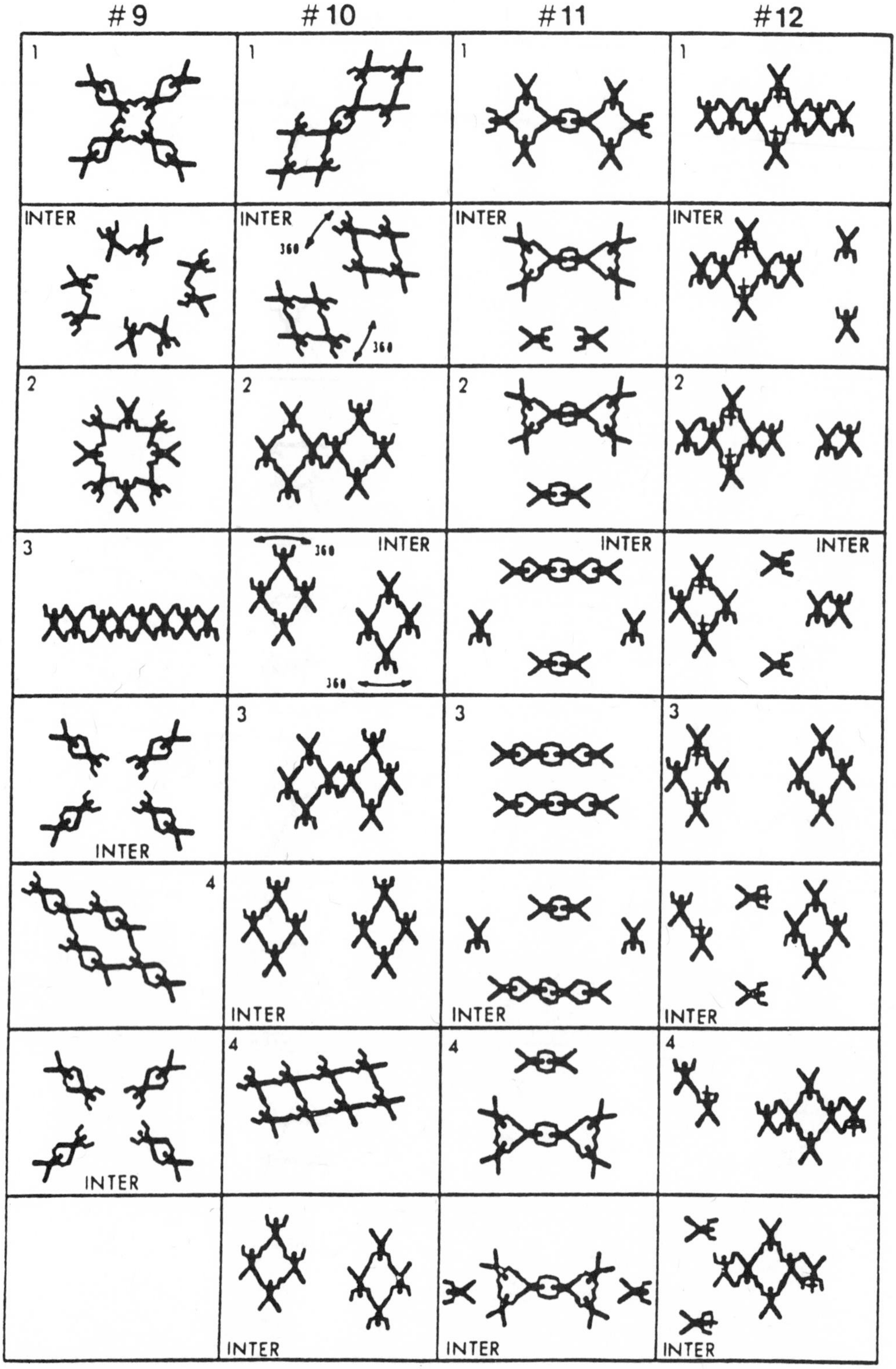

#13   #14   #15

EIGHT-PERSON EVENT RANDOM FORMATIONS

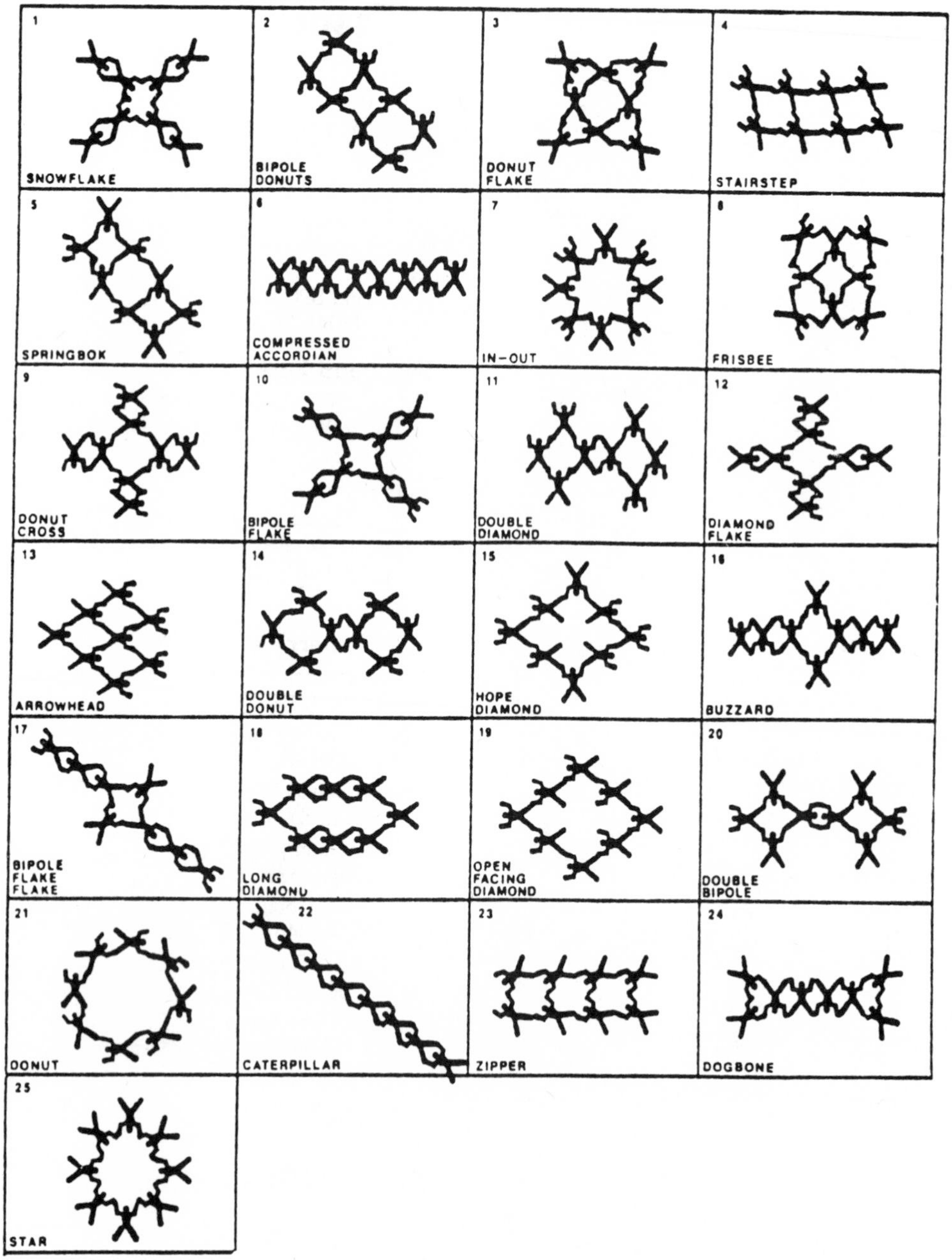

Appendix III

United States Parachute Association Affiliated Centers

The following Sport Parachute Centers are affiliated with the United States Parachute Association. They follow USPA Basic Safety Regulations and Doctrine for student and advanced skydivers. Affiliated Centers also offer first jump courses taught by USPA Certified Instructors.

Central Conference

Archway, 227 N. St., Sparta, IL 62286. (618) 443-2091 or 9020

Cargo-Air SPC, Prairie Lake Lodge, Rt. 2, Marseille, IL 61341

Expert SPC, 4220 N. 11th, Lincoln, NE 68521. (402) 477-5577

First Church of Skydiving, 504 W. Elm St., #5, Urbana, IL 61801. (217) 384-7272

Greene County SPC/Kansas, Rt. 2, Wellsville, KS 66092. (913) 883-2535

Mid-Missouri SPC, Box 206, Moberly, MO 65270. (816) 263-3969

Eastern Conference

Hartwood SPC, Rt. 6, Box 3698. Hartwood, VA 22471. (703) 752-4784

Maytown SPC, 722 Basler Ave., Lemoyne, PA 17043. (717) 255-2292

Parachute Associates Inc., 145 Ocean Ave., Box 811, Lakewood, NJ 08701. (201) 367-7773

Parachutes are Fun, 280 W. State St., Millsboro, DE 19966. (302) 934-8562

Pelicanland Air Sports, RR 1 Box 17, Ridgely, MD 21660. (301) 634-2997

Quantico Skydivers (USMC), Box 344, Quantico, VA 23134

Ripcord Paracenter, Burlington County Airport, Medford, NJ 08055. (609) 267-9897

Southern Cross SPC, Box 366, Williamsport, MD 21795. (301) 223-7541

Sport Parachuting Inc., 300 N. Military Hwy., Norfolk, VA 23502. (804) 461-1500

United Parachute Club, Rt. 663/Swamp Pike, Gilbertsville, PA 19525. (215) 323-9667

West Wind SPC, Box 912, West Point, VA 23181. (804) 785-9990 or 9994

European Parachute League

Hassfurt SPC, 167 A Zollner St., 08600 Bamberg, W. Germany. 0951/3218Z

Illesheim Aero Center, Box 193, APO NY, NY 09140. 09841-8716

Special Forces Europe SPC, Flint Kaserne Bad Toelz, W. Germany. APO NY, NY 09050. 09041-30-616

Mid-Eastern Conference

Air Sports Inc., Branch Airport, Coldwater, MI 49036. (219) 562-3406

Greene County SPC/Gallipolis, Box 91, Bidwell, OH 45614. (614) 245-5011

Greene County SPC/Kentucky, Rt. 2, Box 140, Bardstown, KY 40004. (502) 348-9981

Greene County SPC/Xenia, 1790 Foust Rd., Xenia, OH 45385. (513) 372-6116

Mulenberg County SPC, Box 391, Greenville, KY 42345. (502) 338-0556

Parachuting Service Inc., 197 Burt, Tecumseh, MI 49286. (517) 423-7879

Skydiving Inc., Box 346, Wilmington Air Park, Mason, OH 45040. (513) 398-2955

Waynesville SPC, 4925 N. St. Rt. 42, Waynesville, OH 45088. (513) 897-3851

Mountain Conference

Ogden Sky Knights, Box 9343, Ogden, UT 84409. (801) 392-1557

Reynolds Air Service, Littleton Airport, Sedalia, CO 80135. (303) 794-9390

North Central Conference

Green Bay Skydivers, Carter Airport, Rt. #3, Pulaski, WI 54162. (414) 497-1983 or 822-3644

Kapowsin SPC, 27921 Ort-Kap Hwy., Kapowsin, WI 98344. (206) 893-2907

Minnesota Skydivers, 1200 Tiller Ln., St. Paul, MN 54162. (507) 645-8608

Para Naut, 9096 Hwy. 21, Omro, WI 54963. (414) 685-5995

St. Croix Valley, Box 363, Osceola, WI 54020. (715) 294-2433

Sky Knights, Box 817, E. Troy, WI 53120. (414) 642-9933

So. Wisconsin Skyhawks, 18300 Winfield Rd., Bristol, WI 53104. (414) 857-2007

Valley Parachuting Inc., 630 7th St. W., West Fargo, ND 58078. (701)428-9088

Wisconsin Skydivers, W 204 N 5022 Lannon Rd., Menomonee Falls, WI 53051. (414) 252-9996

Northeastern Conference

Albany Skydiving, Duanesburg Airport, Box 131, Duanesberg, NY 12056. (518) 895-8140

DZ Parachute Club, Fulco Airport, Rt. 67, Johnstown, NY 12095. (518) 762-4900

Frontier Skydivers, 3316 Beebe Rd., Wilson, NY 14172. (716) 751-9981

Gift of Wings, 4539 McKinley Pkwy., Hamburg, NY 14075. (716) 457-9719

Le Jump Pepperell, Rt. 111, Box 601, E. Pepperell, MA 01450. (617) 433-9948

Seneca SPC, RD 2 Box 2632, Seneca Falls, NY 13148. (315) 568-2423

Taunton SPC, 45 Howard St., S. Easton, MA 02375. (617) 823-3682

Wyoming County SPC, RD 1 Box 174A, Arcade, NY 14009. (716) 457-9680

Northwest Conference

Issaquah SPC, 2617 271st St., S.E., Issaquah, WA 98027. (206) 392-2121

Ozmo SPC, Rt. 1, Box 63-S, Athol, ID 83801. (208) 683-2821

Pacific Conference

Corning DZ, Marguerite Ave., Corning, CA 96021. (916) 824-9909

Yolo DZ, 626 Arthur St., Davis, CA 95616. (916) 758-9098

Southeast Conference

Astroid SPC, Box 295, Clemmons, NC 27012. (919) 765-9204 or 622-3618

Carolina Skydivers, Box 786, Shelby, NC 28150. (704) 482-1988

Carolina SPC, Box 21584, Columbia, SC 29221. (803) 798-4346

Central Florida SPC, St. Rt. Box 498A, Eustis, FL 32726. (904) 357-7800

De Land Air Sports, Deland Airport, Box 1657, De Land, FL 32720. (904) 734-5867

E. Carolina Military PC, Box 2032 MCAS, Cherry Point, NC 28533. (919) 466-2667

Fayard Aviation/S. Carolina, Box 236, Moncks Corner, SC 29461. (803) 899-2885

Flying Tigers SPC, Tiger Airport, Clemson, SC 29632. (803) 654-1386

Ft. Gordon SPC, 1924 N. Leg Rd., 8-G, Augusta, GA 30909. (404) 738-0487

Franklin County SPC/Louisburg, Hwy. 56, Box 703, Louisburg, NC 27549. (919) 496-9223

Franklin County SPC/Midland, Midland Field, Hwy. 601, Midland, NC 28107. (704) 888-5479

Greene County SPC/Atlanta, Rt. 4, County Line Rd., Jenkinsburg, GA 30234. (404) 775-9067

Raeford SPC, P.O. Drawer 878, Raeford, NC 28376. (919) 875-3261 or 5626

Skydive Inc., 28700 SW 217th Ave., Homestead, FL 33030. (305) 759-3483 or 274-7526

Swamp Hollow SPC, Rt. 6, Box 13, Quincy, FL 32351. (904) 875-2767

South Florida Parachute, Circle T Ranch Airport, Indiantown, FL 33456. (305) 597-2736

Zephyrhills PC, Box 1101, Zephyrhills, FL 33599. (813) 782-2918

Southern Conference

Central Arkansas SPC, Box 103, Carlisle, AR 72024. (501) 982-4692

Fayard Aviation/Alabama, Box 219, Elberta, AL 36530. (205) 986-8117

Greene County SPC/Louisiana, Rt. 1
Box 667E, Covington, LA 70433.
(504) 892-6311

Southwestern Conference

American Parachute Center, Box 2653,
Bryan, TX 77801. (713) 279-2161

American Parachuting, Ent., 5250 Professional Dr. #54A, Wichita Falls, TX 76302

Houston SPC, 19815 Becker Rd., Hockley,
TX 77447. (713) 351-0194

N. Texas SPC, Barber Airport, Box 2,
Mansfield, TX 76063. (817) 473-0051

Skydance Inc., Tahlequah Municipal Airport,
Tahlequah, OK 74464. (918) 456-5114

Skydivers of Texas, 5301 Parkland Ave.,
Dallas, TX 75235. (214) 824-3540

Spaceland SPC, Houston Gulf Airport,
1525 Pearl, League City, TX 77573.
(713) 337-1713

Western Conference

California City SPC, Box 2178, 6284 Curtis
Place, California City, CA 93505.
(714) 373-4659

Coolidge Parachute Center, Box 1807,
Coolidge, AZ 85228. (602) 723-3753

Elsinore SPC, 20701 Cereal Rd., Elsinore,
CA 92330. (714) 674-2141

Marana Skydiving Center, Marana Airpark,
Marana, AZ 85238. (602) 682-4441

Perris Valley SPC, 2091 S. Goetz Rd., Perris,
CA 92370. (714) 657-3904 or 8727

Taft SPC, 500 Airport Rd., Taft, CA 93268.
(805) 765-6159

APPENDIX IV

DATE 4/11/79   Initiated by: AFS-820

ADVISORY CIRCULAR

DEPARTMENT OF TRANSPORTATION
Federal Aviation Administration
Washington, D.C.

Subject: SPORT PARACHUTE JUMPING

1. <u>PURPOSE</u>. This advisory circular (AC) provides suggestions to improve sport parachuting safety, information to assist parachutists in complying with Federal Aviation Regulations (FAR) Part 105, and a list of aircraft which may be operated with one cabin door removed, including the procedures for obtaining Federal Aviation Administration (FAA) authorization for door removal.

2. <u>CANCELLATION</u>. AC 105-2, Sport Parachute Jumping, dated 9/6/68, is canceled.

3. <u>GENERAL</u>. Sport parachute jumping activities are increasing. While parachutists are not certified airmen, it is recommended that training be conducted as outlined in the United States Parachute Association (USPA) training doctrine or training programs from other similar organizations. Accident statistics have shown that a high percentage of fatal parachute accidents involve student jumpers. During 1976, for example, approximately 42 percent of all parachuting fatalities involved persons who were in training and between their first and 24th jump. These figures indicate that parachutists are exposed to their greatest danger during the process of learning. This AC is designed to assist beginning parachutists and, at the same time, provide helpful information to all other personnel that are involved in sport parachute jumping. In the revision process of this AC, the FAA solicited and received full cooperation and assistance from the USPA and the military services.

4. <u>SAFETY SUGGESTIONS</u>.

    a. <u>Medical</u>. All would-be parachutists are urged to complete a general physical examination prior to their first jump. The physician should be informed of the purpose of the examination.

    b. <u>Initial Training</u>. Prospective parachutists are encouraged to complete a controlled program of instruction prior to attempting a parachute jump. The initial program should cover at least the following areas:

210

(1)   Familiarization with Parachutes.

    (i)   Types to be used.

    (ii)   Main components of the sport parachute.

    (iii)   Function of the sport parachute system.

    (iv)   Fitting the harness.

    (v)   Proper maintenance and care of parachutes.

    (vi)   Canopy control.

    (vii)   Auxiliary parachute.

(2)   Familiarization with the jump aircraft (the best training aid is the jump aircraft).

    (i)   Types used.

    (ii)   Entering procedures.

    (iii)   Seating procedures.

    (iv)   Pre-jump preparation (fitting and attachment of static line, jumpmaster instructions, etc.).

    (v)   Rigging for the jump (buddy system, procedures, etc.).

    (vi)   Exiting from the aircraft.

(3)   Normal Operating Procedures.

    (i)   Verbal count of six seconds after exit to give main parachute time to open.

    (ii)   Check of main chute deploying on count of six or immediately after opening.

    (iii)   Drill on a suspended harness (correcting for malfunctions, dummy ripcord pull of auxiliary chute, etc.).

(4)   Emergency Procedures.

    (i)   Aircraft in-flight emergencies.

    (ii)   Equipment malfunctions.

(iii) Familiarization with the types of reserve chutes (including compatibility with the various types of main chutes).

(iv) Auxiliary chute deployment procedures.

(5) <u>Parachute Landing Falls</u> (preferably from a jump platform).

(i) Types of landing falls.

(ii) Points of body contact.

(iii) Recovery from drags.

(iv) Special landings (tree, high tension wire, water, etc.).

(6) <u>Familiarization with Parachuting Accessories and Instruments.</u>

(i) Altimeters.

(ii) Automatic openers.

(iii) Flotation equipment.

(iv) Personal equipment (boots, goggles, helmets, coveralls, etc.).

(7) <u>Familiarization with Federal Aviation Regulations and Advisory Circulars on Sport Parachuting.</u>

(i) FAR Part 65, Certification: Airmen Other Than Flight Crewmembers.

(ii) FAR Part 91, General Operating and Flight Rules.

(iii) FAR Part 105, Parachute Jumping.

(iv) FAR Part 149, Parachute Lofts.

(v) Technical Standard Order (TSO) C23b, Parachutes.

(vi) AC 65-5A, Parachute Rigger-Senior/Master-Certification Guide.

(vii) AC 149-2H, Listing of Federal Aviation Administration Certification Parachute Lofts.

NOTE: See paragraph 5 for more detailed information.

c. Initial Jumps. Upon completion of a pre-jump instruction program, the following minimum static line jump training is recommended prior to attempting a free-fall jump (if a person has not engaged in parachute jumping activity during the preceding 90 days, static line jumps should be made prior to attempting any free-fall jumps):

(1) At least five static line jumps should be performed from an altitude of at least 2,800 feet above the surface. Low altitude jumps should not be attempted by students.

(2) In order to simulate free-fall type jumps, at least three successive static line jumps should be made during which a dummy ripcord pull is completed prior to opening of the main parachute canopy. These jumps should be accomplished without loss of stability or body control during the fall. (These demonstrations may be accomplished during the five jumps suggested in par. (1) above, or it may be necessary to exceed that number.)

(3) Detailed equipment checks should be made by the jumper prior to each jump. The static line should be checked visually for hookup, and manually by two or three sharp tugs to determine security to the aircraft attaching point. The attachment in the aircraft and the static line attachment should be specifically designed and installed for the purpose intended.

(i) If automatic opening devices are used, a pre-jump check should be made for proper setting, arming, and operational reliability. Devices that depend upon battery power should include periodic check of battery output under a loaded condition. (See par. 4d(2).)

(ii) An experienced parachutist, who acts as the jumpmaster, should make a final inspection of all equipment prior to each jump.

(iii) Complex parachute rigs that require precise action on the part of the jumper should not be used during initial training.

d. Safety Devices and Equipment.

(1) Deployment assist device. Section 105.43(b) of the FAR prohibits any person from making a parachute jump using a static line attached to the aircraft and the main parachute unless an assist device is used to aid the pilot chute in performing its function or, if no pilot chute is used, to aid in the direct deployment of the main parachute canopy.

(2) Automatic opening devices. Although student jumpers seem to feel more at ease if their auxiliary parachutes are equipped with an automatic opening device, recent service experience indicates that such devices may not be completely reliable. Parachute jumpers who elect to use automatic opening devices on the auxiliary parachute should ensure that such devices have been approved by the parachute manufacturer or FAA. The installation of an automatic opening device to a TSO or Military Specification (MIL) -

approved parachute constitutes a major alteration to that parachute. One type of automatic opener utilizes an aneroid type activator which is quite sensitive and could be damaged by a hard fall, or by tossing the parachute into a bin or on a table. Some automatic openers are operated by a timing spring which must be set prior to jumping. These devices are also subject to damage. A parachutist who uses any type of automatic opener should be aware of the reliability aspects of such devices and become very familiar with the device. A complete check of the device and its components should be made prior to each jump to ensure proper functioning. If such devices are used, care must be exercised in setting the minimum opening altitude so as to ensure sufficient time for complete deployment of the auxiliary chute. The jumper should always be prepared to manually pull the ripcord of the auxiliary chute no matter what type of automatic opener is used.

   (3) _Safety equipment_. The area in which jumps are made will indicate the type of safety equipment which should be carried. Each year there are fatalities which resulted from accidental water entries. These deaths were attributed to absence of flotation gear, inability to swim, use of incorrect procedures, and/or extremely cold water. No one should jump without some type of flotation gear except in the few areas where there are absolutely no water-filled ditches or bodies of water in which the jumper could possibly land. Personal gear such as boots, helmets, etc., should be kept in good condition.

   (4) _Oxygen equipment_. Jumpers should use oxygen equipment when the jump aircraft is at altitudes above 10,000 feet MSL (mean sea level) for more than 30 minutes. Oxygen equipment should be used continuously above 15,000 feet MSL. Above 25,000 feet MSL pressure demand oxygen systems should be used.

  e. _Parachute Packing_. Section 105.43(a) permits a parachutist to pack his/her own main chute. Auxiliary parachutes, however, should be packed by a certificated parachute rigger with an appropriate type rating. No alteration or modification can be made to either the main or auxiliary parachute unless it is done by an appropriately certificated parachute rigger or a parachute loft. Even though a jumper can pack his/her own chute, he/she should not attempt to do so until he/she has been thoroughly checked out by a certificated parachute rigger or USPA-certificated instructor.

  f. _Weather_. Strong or gusty winds can be dangerous, especially to student jumpers. Student parachutists should not attempt to make jumps when wind velocities or gusts are such as to impose the risk of injury. In addition, parachutists should ensure there is adequate visibility. (See par. 5c.)

  g. _Advanced Parachuting_. The safety suggestions presented in this circular are intended primarily for the student parachutist. Individual experience and judgment dictate what additional training should be obtained prior to undertaking more advanced parachute activities. Use of high-performance or sophisticated parachute equipment should not be attempted without proper checkout and training. Free-fall acrobatics should be worked up to gradually. High-altitude jumps should not be made without first becoming familiar with the problems and hazards created by low temperatures, lack of oxygen, the various types of oxygen equipment, and under no circumstances attempted without an adequate supply of aviators' breathing oxygen (medical and welding oxygen is unsuitable and could be dangerous).

5. INFORMATION ON REGULATIONS AND ASSOCIATED OPERATING PRACTICES.

a. Federal Aviation Regulations (FAR). The Parts of the FAR which are of interest to parachutists are described below. They may be purchased from the Superintendent of Documents, United States Government Printing Office, Washington, D.C. 20402. Ordering instructions, FAR prices, and stock numbers are contained in AC 00-44, Status of FARs.

(1) Part 65 - Certification: Airmen Other than Flight Crewmembers. Subpart F concerns parachute riggers, their eligibility requirements, privileges, and performance standards.

(2) Part 105 - Parachute Jumping. This Part is especially important to parachutists and to pilots who carry them, since it contains the rules on intentional parachute jumping.

(3) Part 91 - General Operating and Flight Rules. Section 91.15 parachutes and parachuting.

(4) Technical Standard Order (TSO) C23b sets forth the minimum performance and safety requirements for parachutes. TSO C23b is contained in Part 37 of the Federal Aviation Regulations, Section 37.133.

(5) AC 00-44 and this advisory circular may be obtained at no cost by writing the U.S. Department of Transportation, Publications Section, M-443.1, Washington, D.C. 20590.

(6) United States Parachute Association has developed basic safety standards. These are standards for training, checking equipment, and conducting sport parachuting. While not officially approved by the FAA, these standards have been widely used for guidance by individuals and parachute clubs. Copies may be obtained at no cost from the United States Parachute Association, 806 15th Street, N.W., Washington, D.C. 20005.

(7) This circular is based on FAR requirements in effect on the date the circular is published. The FAR may be amended at any time. Parachutists should keep up with changes in the FAR and always comply with current requirements.

b. <u>Parachute Rules</u>. By FAR Part 1 definition, a parachute is a device used or intended to be used to retard the fall of a body or object through the air. For the purposes of this circular, a parachute is an assembly consisting of a harness, canopy, suspension lines, container, ripcord, pilot parachute (if required) and, in some cases, a deployment sleeve or bag. There are, of course, some lesser parts associated with these main components, such as connector links, "D" rings, and pack opening bands. The term "pack" (such as backpack or chestpack), when used in this circular, refers to the parachute assembly, LESS THE HARNESS. This distinction is essential for a clear understanding.

(1) <u>Parachute equipment</u>. FAR 105.43 prescribes that in intentional jumping, the parachutists should wear a single harness dual parachute pack having at least one main parachute and one "approved" auxiliary parachute. The main pack need not be an "approved" pack, but the auxiliary (emergency) pack, the harness, and the auxiliary accessories such as an automatic opening device should always be of an approved type. The following are examples of "approved" parachutes as explained in FAR 105.43(d):

(i) Parachutes manufactured under a type certificate (an early method of approval).

(ii) Parachutes manufactured under TSO C23. These TSO's (TSO C23b is the most recent) prescribe the minimum performance and quality-control standards for a parachute carried for emergency use. These standards are met before the manufacturer labels his/her parachute or components as complying with the TSO.

(iii) Military parachutes (other than high altitude, high speed, or ejection kinds) are identified by an NAF, AAF, or AN drawing number, an AAF order number, or any other military designation or specification number. These parachutes are often referred to as demilitarized or military surplus parachutes.

(iv) Automatic opening devices may be approved as a part of a new production TSO parachute or they may be approved in accordance with procedures described under paragraph (3), Parachute alterations.

(2) <u>Parachute packing</u>. The FARs require the auxiliary parachute to be packed by a certificated parachute rigger or by a certificated and appropriately rated parachute loft. A main parachute may be packed by persons authorized to pack auxiliary parachutes or by the person making the jump; however, the jumper should be thoroughly checked out before attempting to pack his/her parachute. Packing of the main canopy should follow the manufacturer's recommendation.

(3) <u>Parachute alterations</u>. Parachute alterations are changes to original configuration such as the removal of a gore, installation of a light webbing or fitting, addition of a deployment sleeve or bag, changing standard

canopy attachment fittings to quick release fitting, dying of a canopy, alteration of harness, such as changing the ripcord from the left-hand pull to right-hand pull, or the installation of an automatic opening device on an auxiliary parachute. Parachute alterations may be performed only by:

(i) A certificated and appropriately rated master parachute rigger.

(ii) A certificated parachute loft with an appropriate rating.

(iii) Parachute manufacturer.

(iv) Each person listed who alters the auxiliary parachute or the harness of a dual parachute pack used for intentional jumping should do so in accordance with approved manuals and specifications. The method of altering a main parachute does not have to be specifically approved. A person seeking approval to alter an auxiliary parachute should proceed as follows:

(A) The person authorized to alter a parachute (as listed above) should contact the GADO inspector to discuss the proposed modification. The modifier should be prepared to show the inspector the nature of the modification by the use of a sample assembly, a sketch or drawing, and to discuss the nature of the tests that will be needed to demonstrate that the modified parachute meets all requirements.

(B) The inspector will study the proposal with the applicant and a plan of action will be agreed upon.

(C) The applicant will then prepare an application in a letter form, addressed to the local General Aviation District Office (GADO). All pertinent data should be attached. The data should include:

(1) A clear description of the alteration;

(2) Drawings, sketches, or photographs, if necessary;

(3) Information such as thread size, stitch pattern, material used, and location of altered components;

(4) Some means of identifying the altered parachute (model and serial number).

(5) When satisfied, the GADO inspector will indicate approval by date stamping, signing, and placing the GADO identification stamp on the letter of application.

(4) Removal of pilot parachute. A certificated senior or master parachute rigger may remove the pilot chute from an auxiliary parachute.

When this is done, the parachute should be plainly marked "Pilot chute not installed. This parachute may be used for intentional jumping only."

(5) _Extra equipment_. It is not considered to be an alteration when an instrument panel, knife sheath, or other equipment is secured to the pack by passing the pack opening bands through panels or sheath slots.

(6) _Assembly of major parachute components_. The assembly or mating of approved parachute components from different manufacturers may be made by a certificated and appropriately rated parachute rigger or parachute loft without further authorization by the manufacturer or the FAA. Each component of the resulting assembly should function properly and may not interfere with the operation of the other components. For example, a TSO pack may be assembled with a demilitarized harness, or vice versa, as long as the assembled components comply with the safety standards of the original design. Any question about the strength or operation of the assembly should be resolved by actual tests by the rigger or loft to make certain the parachute is safe for emergency use. The user of a single harness dual parachute pack may perform simple assembly and disassembly operations necessary for transportation, handling, or storage between periods of use if the parachute is designed to facilitate such assembly and disassembly without the use of complex operations.

(7) _Repairs_. Parachute repairs can be classed as major repairs or minor repairs. A major repair, as defined in FAR Part 1, is a repair "that, if improperly done, might appreciably affect weight, balance, structural strength, performance, powerplant operation, flight characteristics, or other qualities affecting airworthiness." Other repairs are minor repairs. Major parachute repairs may be made by a master parachute rigger, a parachute loft, or a manufacturer. Examples of major repairs are: replacement of a canopy panel, suspension line, or connector link. Minor parachute repairs may be made by a senior parachute rigger in addition to those authorized to make major repairs. Examples of minor repairs are: replacement of a ripcord pocket, darning, or sewing a small patch on a canopy.

(8) _Plating of fittings_. Plating or replating of load-carrying parachute fittings may cause hydrogen embrittlement and subsequent failure under stress unless the plating is done properly. Chrome or cadmium plated harness adjustment hardware may also have a smoother finish than the original and may permit slippage. The parachutist should be aware of these possible hazards.

c. _Pilot Responsibilities_. The pilot in command of a jump aircraft is solely responsible for certain requirements and jointly responsible for others. The following is a partial list of these requirements:

(1) _Pilot certification and experience requirements_. The pilot is held solely responsible for meeting the certification, proficiency, and experience requirements of Part 61.

(2) <u>Operation requirements</u>. The pilot is responsible for the operation requirement of Part 91 to include the special operating limitations and placards issued for door removal.

(3) <u>Weight and balance procedures</u>. Of paramount importance is the need for the pilot in command to know when his/her aircraft is properly loaded. There can be situations when improper location of jumpers could place the aircraft out of center of gravity (CG) limits. All pilots of aircraft used for sport parachute jumping should give consideration to standard equipment which has been removed (seats and door) and the new empty-weight CG computation. Additional station position information should be provided to the pilot for future weight and balance computations. If this information is not provided, the pilot would experience considerable difficulty in determining actual loaded CG. As a minimum, all aircraft used for sport parachute jumping should contain sufficient information to enable a pilot to compute the aircraft loaded weight and balance.

(4) <u>Jump target zone</u>. It is a good practice for the pilot to make sure that the jump target zone is plainly visible from the aircraft prior to releasing parachutists.

(5) <u>Altitude reporting</u>. Report all altitude to air traffic control in feet above mean sea level (MSL).

(6) <u>Flight visibility and clearance from clouds</u>. The pilot and jumper are jointly responsible for complying with the flight visibility and cloud clearance requirements of Section 105.29. (See App. 1, p.2.)

d. <u>Radio Equipment Requirements</u>. Section 105.14 prescribes the two-way radio communications equipment requirements for aircraft used for parachute jumps in or into controlled airspace unless otherwise authorized by air traffic control. Radio communications should be established with the FAA air traffic control facility or FAA Flight Service Station at least 5 minutes before jumping activity is to begin for the purpose of receiving information on known air traffic in the vicinity of the jump area. Jumping activity cannot begin until this information is received. Additionally, a continuous watch should be maintained on the appropriate frequency until jumping activity is ended. When jumping activities are completed or discontinued, air traffic control should be so informed as soon as possible.

e. <u>Authorization/Notification Requirements</u>. Whether or not written or oral authorization is required for a parachute jump depends upon the type of airspace involved, and the area where the parachutist intends to land. The same criteria determines the type of pre-jump notification requirements. These requirements are explained in detail on page 11. Appendix 1 is an easy reference table parachutists can use to determine what authorization or notification requirements are needed for various types of jumps.

(1) Jumps over or into congested areas or open air assembly of persons. Section 105.15 requires written authorization for these jumps (except for emergencies and certain Armed Forces' operations). Advance application, of at least 4 days, is made by submitting, in triplicate, FAA Form 7711-2, Application for Certificate of Waiver or Authorization, to the FAA General Aviation District Office responsible for the area where the jump is to take place. This rule concerns jumps over or into congested areas or open air assembly of persons. The determination of whether the FAA will authorize the jump will depend on the circumstances of each case. The FAA will not authorize a jump that is hazardous to the public interest. One of the main considerations in granting authorization will be the skill of the parachutist making the jump. The FAA office may stipulate that only a well-qualified jumper may participate in the activity. A demonstration of landing accuracy may be asked for, depending on factors such as the size of the landing area, individual parachutist record, license held, etc. The key to determine if an authorization is or is not necessary is the word "INTO." The following examples may help to clarify the intent of this section and assist in determining when an authorization is necessary:

(i) A jump at a town just east of a large lake. The jumper wishes to exit the aircraft over the lake and drift eastward to land in an open area. NO AUTHORIZATION IS REQUIRED.

(ii) At the same town, the jumpers wish to change the landing site to a school playground in the eastern part of town. The playground is several acres in size, completely fenced in, but surrounded by residential dwellings. Even though the landing target can be placed 500 to 600 feet from the fence, the jump is into a congested area and AUTHORIZATION IS REQUIRED.

(iii) An exhibition jump is planned during the county fair. The fairgrounds are on the north edge of town with clear, open land on three sides. The jumpers plan to exit their aircraft on one side of the fair- ground and land on the opposite side. This is a drift-over jump and an AUTHORIZATION IS NOT REQUIRED.

(iv) At the same fairgrounds, the target is to be placed in the middle of a race track, enclosed by a wire mesh fence and located near the center of the fairgrounds. The target is more than 500 feet from the fence. This would be a jump INTO an open assembly of persons and AUTHORIZATION IS REQUIRED.

(v) Jumps made into large areas, even though near or within a populated area, or near an assembly of persons, do not require written FAA authorization. This provision applies to open areas large enough to enable the parachutist to EXIT the aircraft over the area and REMAIN within the area during descent and landing. Since at no time a jumper would be over anyone on the surface, a jump of this nature would not impose a public hazard. However, parachutists should be careful to completely clear the area of assembly of persons.

(2) <u>Jumps over or onto airports</u>. Section 105.17 requires prior approval of the airport management for jumps made over or onto an airport. However, this does not prevent a parachutist from drifting over an airport without prior approval if the chute is fully deployed and properly functioning and he/she is at least 2,000 feet above the AIRPORT TRAFFIC PATTERN and avoids creating a hazard to air traffic or to persons and property on the surface.

(3) <u>Jumps in or into control zones</u>. Section 105.19 requires an authorization for jumps in or into a control zone with a functioning U.S. operated control tower. Requests for these authorizations do not require a specified lead time, but reasonable notice is desirable so that control tower personnel can adjust the jumps to expected traffic conditions. The authorization and instructions that are issued by the tower for the jumps are based on Visual Flight Rules (VFR) and known air traffic, and do not relieve the parachutists, or the pilot in command of the jump aircraft, from compliance with all air traffic and general operating rules. When jumps in or into control zones involve jumping over or onto an airport, Section 105.17 should also be complied with as explained in paragraph (2) above.

(4) <u>Jumps in or into positive control areas</u>. Section 105.21 prescribes the authorization requirements for parachute jumps in or into positive control areas.

(5) <u>Jumps in or into other airspace</u>. Section 105.23 prescribes the advance notification requirements for parachute jumps in controlled and uncontrolled airspace other than those previously covered in paragraphs (1) through (4). The FAA air traffic control facility or Flight Service Station nearest to the proposed jump site should be notified at least one hour before the jump is to be made, but not more than 24 hours before the jump is to be completed. ATC may accept written notification of a scheduled series of jumps to be made over a stated period of time not to exceed 12 calendar months.

6. <u>AIRCRAFT OPERATING AND AIRWORTHINESS REQUIREMENTS</u>.

a. <u>Procedure</u>. Owners or operators using aircraft listed in Appendix 2 of this AC, and interested in obtaining authorization with operating limitations for operation of such aircraft for parachuting, or other special operations, should forward a written request to the FAA General Aviation District Office having jurisdiction over the area in which such operations are to be conducted. The request should contain the following information:

(1) Name and address of the registered owner of the aircraft.

(2) Make, model, serial and registration number of the aircraft.

(3) Place where the aircraft is normally based.

(4) Reason the aircraft is to be operated with a door removed.

b. <u>List of Eligible Aircraft</u>. Appendix 2 identifies the aircraft which can be operated with one cabin door removed. Other aircraft may be approved for this type of operation if the applicant shows approval by the FAA or the manufacturer.

c. <u>Installation and Removal of Equipment</u>. Removal and installation of equipment will be handled in accordance with the applicable sections of FAR 43. The original conversion to the jump configuration should be performed by an appropriately certificated person and recorded in the aircraft records. The equipment list and weight and balance data should be revised to show both the jump configuration and the normal configuration. Subsequent conversions may be made by the pilot if the work falls within the scope of preventive maintenance (see FAR Part 43, Appendix A(c)).

d. <u>Office of Management and Budget (OMB 04-R0140)</u>. The reporting and/or recordkeeping requirements contained in this paragraph (paragraph 6) have been approved by the Office of Management and Budget in accordance with the Federal Reports Act of 1942.

J. A. FERRARESE
Acting Director
Flight Standards Service

TABLE OF LOCATION OF JUMP/AUTHORIZATION/NOTIFICATION

Location of Jump	Kind of Authorization or Approval Required	When to Apply or Notify	Where to Obtain or Give Notice	FAR Reference
Over or into congested areas or open air assembly of persons.	Certificate of authorization	Apply at least 4 days before the jump	FAA General Aviation or Flight Standards District Office	105.15
Over or onto an airport with or without a U.S. operated control tower.	Prior Approval	Apply before jump	Airport Management	105.17
In or into control zone with a U.S. operated control tower.	Authorization 1/	Apply before jump	Control Tower 2/	105.19
In or into positive control area 3/.	Authorization 1/	Apply before jump	Nearest ATC facility or FSS 2/	105.21
In or into other controlled airspace.	None	Notify before jump	Nearest ATC facility or FSS at least 1 hour before but not more than 24 hours before jumping is to be completed 2/	105.23
In or into uncontrolled airspace.	None	Notify before jump	Same as above except 2/ does not apply	105.23
Over or within restricted or prohibited.	Authorization 1/	Apply before jump	The agency in charge of the area	105.27

1/ Verbal authorization normally issued.
2/ Communication required with nearest FAA ATC or FSS 5 minutes before jump.
3/ Positive control area begins at 18,000 feet and extends upward to 60,000 feet.

NOTE: This table does not apply to jumps by the Armed Forces over or within restricted areas that are under the control of an Armed Force or during military operations in uncontrolled airspace.

Information Required for Notification. (FAR 105.25)

1. Date and time jumping will begin.
2. Size of the jump zone in nautical miles (radius around target).
3. Location of jump zone related to the nearest VOR radial or nearest airport, town, or city.
4. Altitudes above the surface at which jumping will take place.
5. Time and duration of the intended jumping.
6. Name, address, and telephone number of the person requesting the authorization or giving notice.
7. Identification of the aircraft to be used.
8. Radio frequencies, if any, available in the aircraft.

NOTE: Although not specifically required by all authorization and notification sections of FAR 105, the FAA recommends that proposed jump areas be coordinated with the nearest ATC facility for advisory information concerning other airspace operations.

Clearance-From-Clouds Requirements and Visibility Minimum. (FAR 105.29)

More than 1,200 feet above the surface and at or above 10,000 feet MSL: 1,000 feet under, 1,000 feet over, 1 mile horizontally from clouds. Flight visibility 5 miles.

Elsewhere: 500 feet under, 1,000 feet over, 2,000 feet horizontally from clouds.
Flight visibility 3 miles.

NOTE: NO PERSON MAY MAKE A PARACHUTE JUMP INTO OR THROUGH A CLOUD.

"Controlled Airspace" means airspace, designated as continental control area, control area, control zone, terminal control area or transition area, within which some or all aircraft may be subject to air traffic control. (FAR 1.1)

Parachute Equipment and Packing Requirements for Intentional Jumping. (FAR 105.43)

The parachutist should wear a single harness dual parachute pack, having at least one main parachute and one approved auxiliary parachute. The main parachute should have been packed by a certificated parachute rigger, or by the person making the jump, within 120 days before its use. The auxiliary parachute should have been packed by a certificated and appropriately rated parachute rigger within 120 days when constructed of synthetic fiber, and 60 days when constructed of natural fiber material such as silk.

OFFICE OF MANAGEMENT AND BUDGET (OMB 04-R0147). The reporting and/or recordkeeping requirements contained in Appendix 1 have been approved by the Office of Management and Budget in accordance with the Federal Reports Act of 1942.

AIRCRAFT THAT MAY BE OPERATED WITH ONE CABIN DOOR REMOVED

Aeronca 05B

Aeronca 15AC

Beech AT-11, 18 Series,
  C-45 and TC-45 Series

Centaur 101

Cessna 120 Series

Cessna 140 Series

Cessna 150 Series

Cessna 170 Series

Cessna 172 Series

Cessna 175 Series

Cessna 180 Series

Cessna 182 Series

Cessna 185 Series

Cessna 190

Cessna 206 Series (with Cessna
  Accessory Kit AK 206-1 installed)

Cessna 210 Series

Cessna (Ector) 305A

Champion (Aeronca) 7 Series

Curtiss Wright (Travel Air)
  S-6000B

Douglas DC-3 (Maximum airspeed cabin
  passenger door removed 170 knots)

Fairchild 24 Series (R/H door)

Helio H 250

Helio H 295

Helio H 391

Helio H 395

Howard DGA-15 Series

Larson (Luscombe) 8 Series (R/H
  door - maximum airspeed 100 MPH)

Lockheed Model 12A

Lockheed 402-2 (R/H rear door)

Macchi AL 60 (R/H rear door)

Noorduyn UC-64 Series (rear door)

Piper PA-12

Piper PA-18 Series

Piper PA-20 Series

Piper PA-22 Series

Piper PA-28-140-160-180-235

Stinson V-77

Stinson Jr. SR-4

Stinson SR-7B (R/H door)

Taylorcraft BC 12-D

Temco (Luscombe) 11A (R/H door)

Universal (Stinson) 108 Series

NOTE: Some of the above aircraft may require installation of deflectors to
        reduce vibration while being operated with a door removed.

AIRCRAFT THAT MAY BE OPERATED WITH ONE CABIN DOOR REMOVED

Aeronca 05B

Aeronca 15AC

Beech AT-11, 18 Series, C-45 and TC-45 Series

Centaur 101

Cessna 120 Series

Cessna 140 Series

Cessna 150 Series

Cessna 170 Series

Cessna 172 Series

Cessna 175 Series

Cessna 180 Series

Cessna 182 Series

Cessna 185 Series

Cessna 190

Cessna 206 Series (with Cessna Accessory Kit AK 206-1 installed)

Cessna 210 Series

Cessna (Ector) 305A

Champion (Aeronca) 7 Series

Curtiss Wright (Travel Air) S-6000B

Douglas DC-3 (Maximum airspeed cabin passenger door removed 170 knots)

Fairchild 24 Series (R/H door)

Helio H 250

Helio H 295

Helio H 391

Helio H 395

Howard DGA-15 Series

Larson (Luscombe) 8 Series (R/H door – maximum airspeed 100 MPH)

Lockheed Model 12A

Lockheed 402-2 (R/H rear door)

Macchi AL 60 (R/H rear door)

Noorduyn UC-64 Series (rear door)

Piper PA-12

Piper PA-18 Series

Piper PA-20 Series

Piper PA-22 Series

Piper PA-28-140-160-180-235

Stinson V-77

Stinson Jr. SR-4

Stinson SR-7B (R/H door)

Taylorcraft BC 12-D

Temco (Luscombe) 11A (R/H door)

Universal (Stinson) 108 Series

NOTE: Some of the above aircraft may require installation of deflectors to reduce vibration while being operated with a door removed.

Readers wishing more information are urged to purchase a copy of *The Parachutist Guidebook* published by the United States Parachute Association, Suite 444, 806 15th Street, N.W., Washington, D.C. 20005.

Index